Do you believe it is possib̲ and depression? In *Choosing a Way Out*, you will walk with Kirsten Samuel and her husband, Dave, through the pain and reality of a secret life that threatened to end their marriage. The Samuels reveal how redemption and reconciliation are possible when you submit to God's Plan. As you read their story, you'll find hope for the wounds you carry as you learn a proven method to heal from devastating lies and step into faith-filled freedom.

Joanne F. Miller
author of *Creating a Haven of Peace*

As a pastor, I see the devastation pornography and depression causes to individuals, marriages, and families. It's not something we choose to talk about often, but it is real and destroying lives and marriages. This book, *Choosing a Way Out*, chooses to tackle these subjects carefully and honestly. In reading through David and Kirsten's story, you will see how God provides redemption and reconciliation when we are willing to submit to Him. You will journey with them and their amazing Restoration Team through the pain to restoration. Life is messy. Yet God restores beauty from the messiness.

Brady Boyd
Senior Pastor, New Life Church

*Choosing a Way Out* is an insightful look at David and Kirsten's journey and struggles together and the good news of redemption and healing through Christ. This book gives hope and help to anyone facing a similar journey.

Garvin McCarrell
Sr Executive Pastor, New Life Church

*Choosing a Way Out* walks you through the experience of a devoted Christian couple who find their family suddenly shipwrecked by pornography. Feel the desperation of trying to protect a well-crafted image for others to admire. Connect the dots between unresolved childhood trauma and anxiety disorder and PTSD. Imagine what it's like to have a son ask, "Do you love my dad?" and to struggle to say 'no' to divorce, and 'yes' to God, her husband, and their wedding vows. Read the story of how the author learned to unlock her repressed grief and found answers at the bottom of that deep pit. Learn the hope found in a Christ-centered restoration team and marriage counselor, and the breakthroughs and restoration of trust, friendship, and intimacy. Finally, mine the resources at the end of their story, and discover that these alone are worth the price of the book.

Rob Jackson, MS, LPC,
ChristianCounsel

In *Choosing a Way Out*, Kirsten Samuel walks you through the devastation years of hidden lies wrought on her marriage, her emotions, her mind, and her physical body. With delicate dealing of difficult topics, the author points us to a way out that resulted in complete restoration, continued healing, and courageous authentic living. Engagingly written, you will find yourself and your story in these pages along with hope in God's restoration and redemption.

Stephanie Henderson
Executive Pastor, New Life Church, and
author of *Her Heart Is Torn*

So raw, so real, so insightful and well written. As you read their story, you'll find hope for the wounds you carry. *Choosing a Way Out* will inspire you to new levels.

Scott & Bethany Palmer
*The Money Couple, www.themoneycouple.com*

From Broken to Healed:

Kirsten Samuel's poignant story of her personal journey through the crisis of her husband's addiction to pornography is both touching and inspiring. The raw honesty with which she and Dave share their story brought tears to my eyes, but it also gave me hope that there is absolutely nothing that we can't face when we allow Jesus to take the lead. Regardless of the crisis you may be facing, this book is a must read because the core answer is the same for all of us – allow Jesus to affect the healing.

Fran Veal
Author of the *Finding My Escape* novels

Kirsten, and her husband Dave, beautifully tell their story of the devastating years of lies. As you walk through the pages of *Choosing a Way Out*, you'll see God's restoration and redemption over addiction, depression, and the resulting devastation on their marriage, as well as the author's emotions, mind, and physical body. I think you'll find yourself in these pages as I did. But, more than anything, you'll find hope in a God who restores and redeems.

Yvette Maher
Dream Centers CDO and
Author of *My Hair and God's Mercies...New Every Morning*

Betrayed. Wounded. Forever changed.

*Choosing a Way Out: When the Bottom isn't the Bottom* is more than a book about one couple's road to recovery and redemption. It's a guide to healing. Both Kirsten and her husband share from their hearts and their hurts.

Through Biblical counsel and example, tears and trials, this book is an encouraging tool for those who have had the bottom fall out.

*Choosing a Way Out* is a real life reminder that we always have a choice no matter how difficult it may be, how far off it may seem, how much we may not want to admit our part.

If you are looking for hope and are willing to do the work, if you are open to a triumph through your trial, allow Choosing a Way Out to be a part of your journey to a new normal.

Daphne V. Smith
www.welldonelife.com

It's real, it's raw, and it gets your attention. It's also hopeful. It shows the process of healing with God...that we can't do it on our own and how powerfully God works in our innermost beings to restore us.

Kristie Tamillow
www.bestbabysleepsolutions.com

# Choosing a Way Out

# Other books by Kirsten Samuel

5 Lies Moms Believe

# Choosing a Way Out

## When the Bottom Isn't the Bottom

**Kirsten Samuel**

**Foreword by** Kary Oberbrunner
Author of *ELIXIR Project, Day Job to Dream Job,*
*The Deeper Path,* and *Your Secret Name*

Printed in the United States of America

Published by Author Academy Elite
P.O. Box 43, Powell, OH 43035
www.AuthorAcademyElite.com

All Scripture quotations, unless otherwise indicated, are taken from the *Holy Bible*, New International Version®, NIV®. Copyright ©1973, 1978, 1984, 2011 by Biblica, Inc.™ Used by permission of Zondervan. All rights reserved worldwide. www.zondervan.com The "NIV" and "New International Version" are trademarks registered in the United States Patent and Trademark Office by Biblica, Inc.™

Scripture quotations marked THE MESSAGE are taken from *THE MESSAGE*, copyright © 1993, 1994, 1995, 1996, 2000, 2001, 2002 by Eugene H. Peterson. Used by permission of NavPress. All rights reserved. Represented by Tyndale House Publishers, Inc.

Scripture quotations marked *NLT* are taken from the *Holy Bible*, New Living Translation, copyright ©1996, 2004, 2007, 2013, 2015 by Tyndale House Foundation. Used by permission of Tyndale House Publishers, Inc., Carol Stream, Illinois 60188. All rights reserved.

Listening to God Guidelines © 2004 by PRT of The Navigators. Used by permission of The Navigators. All rights reserved.

Inner Healing Guidelines © 2004 by PRT of The Navigators. Used by permission of The Navigators. All rights reserved.

The Internet addresses, email addresses, and phone numbers in this book are accurate at the time of publication. They are provided as a resource. Kirsten Samuel or the publisher do not endorse them or vouch for their content or permanence.

Paperback ISBN: 978-1-946114-48-8
Hardcover ISBN: 978-1-946114-49-5

Library of Congress Control Number: 2017903435
Author Academy Elite, Powell, OHIO

Cover design: 99designs.com/poppins
Author Photography: Blain Andersen

Also available in hardcover, softcover, e-book, and audiobook.

*For Peter, Debbie, Ken, Jackie, Rick, and Cathy who exemplify what it means to be "Jesus with skin on."*

*You rescued, protected, admonished, and encouraged us to be more than we were. Thank you for believing for, and in, us when we didn't believe there was a way out.*

Everyone says forgiveness is a lovely idea, until they have something to forgive.

C.S. Lewis

# Contents

Foreword . . . . . . . . . . . . . . . . . . . . . . . . . . . . . . . . . . xv
When Grace Begins . . . . . . . . . . . . . . . . . . . . . . . . . . 1

## The Crisis

When You Stumble Over What's Hidden . . . . . . . . . . . 7
When You Step In It . . . . . . . . . . . . . . . . . . . . . . . . . 15
When There's Nowhere To Hide. . . . . . . . . . . . . . . . . 23
When It's Not So Happily Ever After . . . . . . . . . . . . . 27
When The Jig Is Up. . . . . . . . . . . . . . . . . . . . . . . . . . 35
When It's Not Up To You . . . . . . . . . . . . . . . . . . . . . 41
When Friends Believe For You . . . . . . . . . . . . . . . . . 45
When They "Get You" Before You Get You . . . . . . . . . 49
When You Make The Team You Don't Want. . . . . . . . . 53

## The Choice

When You Don't Know If You Want To Be Whole. . . . . 59
When It Starts With Commitment. . . . . . . . . . . . . . . . 65
When You Realize Commitment Means
        You Have No Control. . . . . . . . . . . . . . . . . . . . . 69
When You Start To Wonder If
        You Can Do Anything Right. . . . . . . . . . . . . . . . . 77
When You Have To Decide If You Do Or You Don't . . . 83
When You Hear Your Son Say, "Do You Love My Dad?" . . . 93

## The Community

When You Discover You Were Never Alone . . . . . . . . 99
When You Think You Have Nothing To Hide . . . . . . . . 103

When You're Pointing A Finger
    In The Wrong Direction . . . . . . . . . . . . . . . . . . . .109
When You're The Last One To Know . . . . . . . . . . . . .117
When You Rip Off The Scab . . . . . . . . . . . . . . . . . . .121
When You Think You Want To Die. . . . . . . . . . . . . . .127
When You Are Surprised By Kindness. . . . . . . . . . . .129
When Nothing Makes Sense. . . . . . . . . . . . . . . . . . .133
When You Have To Wake Up. . . . . . . . . . . . . . . . . . .139
When Death Smacks You In The Face . . . . . . . . . . . .145
When Too Much Happens At Once. . . . . . . . . . . . . .149
When You Aren't Prepared . . . . . . . . . . . . . . . . . . . .153
When The Past Heals The Present . . . . . . . . . . . . . .161
When Jesus Redeems Your Past . . . . . . . . . . . . . . . .171
When You Learn To Grieve. . . . . . . . . . . . . . . . . . . .177
When Healing Requires Remembering . . . . . . . . . . .183
When There Were Two In The Moonlight . . . . . . . . .189
When Unresolved Issues Reveal The Darkness. . . . . .195
When The Answer Comes At The Bottom . . . . . . . .201

**The Covenant**

When Hurt Becomes Healing. . . . . . . . . . . . . . . . . .207
When Beauty Awakens . . . . . . . . . . . . . . . . . . . . . . .215
When You Are Completely Known And Fully Loved. . .219
When You Choose To Begin Again. . . . . . . . . . . . . . .223
When You Realize Covenant
    Is More Than A Contract. . . . . . . . . . . . . . . . . . . .229
When You Learn To Take Him At His Word. . . . . . . .235
When Your Trust Is Tested. . . . . . . . . . . . . . . . . . . .241
When You Choose Integrity . . . . . . . . . . . . . . . . . . .245
When You Choose The Open Door . . . . . . . . . . . . .249
When Grace Wins . . . . . . . . . . . . . . . . . . . . . . . . . .261

# Appendix

The ABC's of My Position . . . . . . . . . . . . . . . . . . . . . 267

Depression Signs and Symptoms. . . . . . . . . . . . . . . 268

Who Can I Call For Help? . . . . . . . . . . . . . . . . . . . . 272

Signs Someone You Love Is Addicted. . . . . . . . . . . . . 276

Questions To Ask If You Think Someone
    You Love Is Addicted To Pornography . . . . . . . . . 279

Inner Healing And Listening To God Guidelines . . . . . 280

How To Journal . . . . . . . . . . . . . . . . . . . . . . . . . . . . 282

Helpful Questions To Ask Each Other. . . . . . . . . . . . 286

Where Can I Go To Learn More About God?. . . . . . . 289

Scripture Verses Helpful For Dealing With
    Depression And Anxiety . . . . . . . . . . . . . . . . . . . 290

Resources . . . . . . . . . . . . . . . . . . . . . . . . . . . . . . . . 298

Endnotes. . . . . . . . . . . . . . . . . . . . . . . . . . . . . . . . . 303

Acknowledgements. . . . . . . . . . . . . . . . . . . . . . . . . . 311

About The Author. . . . . . . . . . . . . . . . . . . . . . . . . . 313

# Foreword

Every so often you hear a story that at first seems unbelievable.

That's how I felt when I heard David and Kirsten's story. To see them today, you wouldn't suspect the deep crisis that occurred a few years earlier. Yet when I heard the beginning of the story, I saw God's redemption being lived out.

In *Choosing a Way Out: When the Bottom Isn't the Bottom*, Kirsten Samuel walks us through the day that forever changed both of them. As you journey through the pages of their story, you will find hope that life can indeed be redeemed no matter how dark it seems.

*Think you can't survive pornography addiction?* In their story you'll find hope, humility, forgiveness, and God's redemptive work. You can overcome any stronghold and live with integrity once again.

*Believe that depression means you will never experience joy again?* Walk with the author as she uncovers the lies of her depression and discovers God's Truth to eventually live in freedom and joy.

*Convinced that your marriage cannot recover from the lies of the past?* Discover anew, or maybe for the first time, the meaning of covenant and the hope found when we submit first to God and then to each other.

This book offers you a way out of the pit. It offers hope, not clichés. It presents truth from God's Word, if you are willing to believe and apply it. It shows a way to find freedom from the prison of lies you've believed, if you are willing to embrace the pain, open yourself to God's Word, and admit you are in need of healing, just like your partner.

God will make all things new if we choose to walk through the pain.

Kary Oberbrunner
Author of *Elixir Project, Day Job to Dream Job, The Deeper Path,* and *Your Secret Name*

# When Grace Begins

*You may slip—indeed you will—but you will not fall.*
Max Lucado

There are times in life when you are blindsided. Nothing prepares you for the cataclysmic event coming your way.

I suppose it's a good thing we can't see the future because if we could, we would probably opt out.

At some point we all face our worst fears. Some fears are worse than others—but in this life we can't escape them completely.

I came face-to-face with a fear I didn't even know to consider when my carefully crafted world shattered almost a decade ago. That awful day is forever branded on my mind, seared so I will never forget.

But discovering Dave's hidden addiction was not the only thing I discovered that day.

It was on that day I began to discover the extent of my deception. The prison of lies I built. Carefully constructed over years and years. Reinforced, patched up, and reinforced again to protect myself.

Digging through my cluttered mind for answers, I saw the thread of lies I crafted and believed.

- Lies to protect myself.
- Lies to protect others from the truth.
- Lies to maintain my self-image.
- Lies to bolster my self-image.

Lies.

I would list more, but I've lost track of all the distortions. They make me weary from the weight of carrying them.

Believing the lie that I had to be all things to all people, I went out of my way to make sure everyone around me was happy. I wouldn't confront when someone placed unnecessary blame on me. Instead I'd assume it was my fault and make the required correction.

The lies seemed to be stored on tapes in my mind. The tapes would play regularly reminding me of all I needed to protect, to maintain my image, to give me value. Some were quite clever, about one degree off of the truth. You know the kind—"little white lies." The kind meant to protect others from a sting of pain and make us look good. Lies meant to appear as truth but are not the full truth. Lies to save face.

Then there were the lies in my actions. "Do you want to help me with this project?" "Sure I do," I answered when it was honestly the last thing in the world I wanted. "You're

so good at this, I know you should be in charge." Not really.
I just fake being good at it. I fake it well.

At least, until now.

Thus began my journey into my darkest place. A journey
into darkness, my self-constructed prison, and, eventually,
my freedom.

One day my story, the one I'd authored with a golden pen,
began to shift. I began to see the gilded castle I'd built for
myself, and my family, was actually a prison. A prison I'd built.
Not a physical building or space, but a secretly constructed
series of mental walls and chains, vows and lies designed to
protect my wounded heart. Wounds so deep I couldn't bear
to look at them. Walls so high I thought I'd never escape.
The words swirled in my clouded mind:

Don't think. Don't feel. Don't remember.
Stay in the shadows.
Forget and keep moving.
Hide.
People pleaser.
Tough girl.
Who am I?
Why am I still alive?

Darkness so deep I'm no longer seen, or can see.

But then I see.

My eyes strain to focus—the light hurts.

Is it the jailor? Is it my silent accuser?

No. It's Jesus.

My heart breathes His name. Jesus. Arms open wide, He softly begins to sing His love song for me. Gently He sings as the walls begin to crumble.

For the first time I believe it is possible to be free.

> Come back to the place of safety, all you prisoners who still have hope!
>
> I promise this very day that I will repay two blessings for each of your trouble.[1]

# The Crisis

# When You Stumble Over What's Hidden

*I will not die; instead, I will live to tell what the LORD has done.*

*Psalm 118:17 NLT*

I was totally unaware of the imminent crisis. It had been an uneventful day. An ordinary, comfortable, predictable day. A typical Monday workday—catching up on email, planning the various tasks for the rest of the week, attending several meetings to prepare for the upcoming fall. School would be starting soon so we were in final planning mode at the office.

For once, I actually left work on time to get home and finish dinner before Dave walked in the door. Our oldest son, Eric, who was finishing up the last few weeks of work before he headed off to college, would also be hungry.

That night Dave was unusually quiet at dinner and didn't eat very much, saying he wasn't hungry. I thought it strange but perhaps he'd eaten a late lunch.

After I cleaned up the dinner dishes, I noticed Dave had gone to our bedroom and was lying down on the bed, which was odd for that time of evening. As I approached, I could tell he was very upset. Without raising his head from the pillow, he quietly informed me that it was very likely he would be fired.

Sinking quickly onto the other side of the bed, I asked, "Why?"

With no trace of color in his face he responded, "Because of a moral failure."

I couldn't breathe. It felt like the air was sucked out of the room.

With a calmness that had to come from the Holy Spirit, I asked a few more questions and listened as he revealed his lifelong struggle.

I heard only one word. "Pornography."

And my world shattered.

Haltingly, brokenly, he spoke of his hidden addiction. I don't remember his words.

My husband of 25 years worked for an international Christian ministry. Being a faith organization they, obviously, took a hard stand against the evils of pornography. Thoughts tumbled through my brain like,

*"He was doing this at work?" "How long has this been going on?"*

He'd been hiding this addiction for years. Now he'd been caught—at work—and the consequences were probably going to be severe.

I'd never seen his face so distraught or heard such anguish in his voice. He stumbled over his words, his whole body shaking with shame. He was devastated, horrified at what he'd done—to me, to our marriage, to himself.

Dave went on to explain that there would be a meeting the next day to determine if he could keep his job. At that meeting, he was to present a game plan of how he would deal with this addiction—not only deal with it but get rid of it. He didn't sense much hope of retaining his job. The company's policy was very clear: "Grounds for immediate dismissal."

The night suddenly took a sharp left turn. What should have been the time to begin our evening bedtime routine was now not even a conceivable thought. I felt my body respond in full crisis mode. Adrenaline pumped through me while my brain felt sluggish. I felt as if I was sprinting through tall grass trying to escape a roaring lion, and yet I couldn't move. I had no way to process this revelation.

Instead my mind jumped from fragment to fragment, nothing making a connection. The pain and confusion was so intense it felt like I would explode into a million pieces at any moment. I desperately tried to remain calm and rational, but my shaking body betrayed me.

I was stunned, hurt, angry, shocked, and in complete disbelief. I couldn't wrap my mind around what was happening to my perfect world, my wonderful marriage. My gilded castle.

Sleep was the furthest thing from my mind, when he said, "I completely understand if you want me to sleep on the couch."

I heard myself say, "Well, it'll be crowded with the two of us."

Humor and levity, usually welcome in our marriage, came from somewhere inside me. A totally surprising comment to come out of my mouth at that moment, especially since sleeping wasn't on my radar in the foreseeable future. The compassion in my statement was completely out of sync with my ricocheting emotions and felt as if it came from some other world.

*"Who is this man in our house?"*

The thought flitted through my head that I didn't know this man I'd been married to for a quarter of a century. How could this be? He's such a "good" man. How? What now?

I knew we needed help, but I didn't know where to turn.

Before either of us could consider sleep of any kind, we knew we had to tell our three kids. If a job termination was imminent, they needed to know from us. How would it be to hear, out of the blue, that your dad suddenly lost his job?

So, instead of starting our bedtime routine, Dave went downstairs to tell our son, Eric. I stayed in our room. Reeling from the news.

To make matters even more delicate, Dave and Eric worked at the same company. Dave's co-workers were Eric's co-workers. He would be greatly impacted by the scandal of this announcement, so he needed to know right away.

As reality began to set in so did my pain and disgust.

While Dave was talking with our son, the phone rang. It was our son-in-law, Casey. He also worked at the same ministry with Dave. He'd seen Dave at work and thought something was wrong. He called to make sure Dave was okay. I carried the phone toward our son's room where I heard murmuring voices. After handing the phone to Dave, he asked Casey to put our daughter, Erin, on the phone too.

With a hollow voice he explained the situation to our daughter and new husband. His colorless face reflected the agony in his soul. Almost devoid of emotion, he spoke quietly while I sat in a nearby chair, thoughts whirling, scrambling to make some sense of the last half hour. Part of me ached for his pain, while another part took secret satisfaction in it.

Eric, Casey, and Erin extended immediate forgiveness to Dave and said they would stand by him no matter what. They knew and loved Dave for the wonderful, caring, creative father he had always been to them. In their minds, this addiction did not define him.

Our youngest son, Nate, was overseas at university at the time. In the next few days, Dave would email him to let him know that he needed to talk with him as soon as possible.

Out of the blue, a thought came to mind. In what can only be the intervention of the Holy Spirit at this time of confusion and crisis, I had a crystal clear thought. One of my dear co-workers and her husband were trained counselors. We should call them.

The boulder growing in the pit of my stomach seemed to shove me into action. We needed help and we needed it now. I asked Dave if he was willing to meet with them immediately if they were available. Tonight. He agreed. It was late, but I made the call. They agreed to meet with us right away. They wanted to see us in person.

I felt dead inside as we drove to meet them. There were no words. I was stunned. And reeling.

We walked into the building, where at the first sight of my co-worker, I erupted in tears. Agonizing, hot tears of confusion, anger, and pain flooded my face.

"Where were my tissues?"

They ushered us into a meeting room. We sat there. Probably as a natural impulse, Dave wanted to hold my hand. I didn't want to touch him.

Dave told his story to Cathy and Rick. They listened, asked a few questions, and then turned to me, a puddle of tears. I don't recall everything that was said, but the one question I remember asking them over and over was, "Why didn't I know?"

Their answer, "You did. At some level."

My heart slipped beyond what I had earlier believed was its lowest point and crashed. Splintering into pieces. Rock bottom. Had I known and refused to acknowledge the pornography?

Such an ugly word. Such ugly images filled my mind.

We discussed the ultimatum at his job. They suggested he submit to counseling and suggested we also needed marriage counseling.

> "You can get over this addiction. It's not fatal."

Their next words brought the first hope—a ray of warm light into a dark, cold place. "You can get over this addiction. It's not fatal." We both needed to hear that.

We drove home in silence.

As the boulder in my gut continued to push, I asked Dave to call two of the men from our couple's Bible study. He did. He scheduled breakfast the next day with Peter, one of the men Dave had known for 15 years.

I didn't sleep much that night. I prayed a lot and wrestled with my emotions. Not long into the dark night I realized I was very angry. I'd gone beyond hurt to angry. I could feel myself shaking. Yet, in the midst of this emotional turmoil, the Father reminded me of Himself.

*Taste and see that the LORD is good; blessed is the one who takes refuge in him. Fear the LORD, you his holy people, for those who fear him lack nothing. The lions may grow*

*weak and hungry, but those who seek the LORD lack no good thing.*[1]

However, what I didn't know was that I was deeply grieving. Grieving the loss of the marriage I thought was so good and the man I thought I'd married.

# When You Step In It

*I'll never forget the trouble, the utter lostness, the taste of ashes, the poison I've swallowed.*
*Lamentations 3:19 THE MESSAGE*

D ave's confession caught me totally off guard. Way, way off guard! Because the addiction Dave revealed was a dichotomy. He couldn't be doing that. He was not that kind of guy. He was a sincerely loving, attentive husband from the moment we married. The juxtaposition of his revelation and my daily reality was implausible.

There's more to this story, but it is better you hear it from Dave.

## Dave

I've always been a sensitive sort. Throughout the years, I felt like I was different or something was wrong with me, more often than not. While I wanted to play sports well, like the other guys, the truth is

I was mediocre at best. Plus, I wasn't all that interested in sports like most of my male peers.

I was interested in how things were made—I guess that makes me more of a "creative" type of guy.

Add this creative bent to my natural inclination to not look foolish, and I spent a lot of time in my own head. I tended to spend more time observing the world around me and others' behavior than asking questions. My silence further emphasized my introspection.

Being alone with your thoughts can be creative and productive...but not always.

My first exposure to pornography occurred around six years old. My folks sent my brother and me to the barbershop, a few blocks from our home, to get our hair cut.

As was typical at the time, there was a magazine rack on the wall. The way they were arranged, you could only see the titles. Because I was just learning how to read, I saw the word "play" and "boy" which I recognized. I don't remember thinking anything about it other than I was a boy and liked to play games and play outside.

Since this was in the '60's, there wasn't a lot of fleshly exposure on magazine covers. But for some reason I remained curious about that "boy playing," so I pulled the unfamiliar magazine out of the rack.

That's when I saw my brother shaking his head, motioning and mouthing the words, "Put it back. Put it down."

The barber smiled at me and gave me raised eyebrows along with a grin that seemed to say, "Heh, heh, heh, 'atta boy." I thought, "Why was he pleased at what I saw?" I quickly put it back and sat down. I was very confused. And embarrassed. I didn't talk to anyone about it.

For some reason, as a young child I was very curious about my body and how bodies work. I wondered:

- How does the blood get around the body?
- Are there little people pushing things around?
- How do my muscles work?
- If I swallow a watermelon seed will one grow in my stomach?
- What really happens when you go to the bathroom?
- How does white milk turn into yellow pee?

Perhaps this curiosity was fueled by the images I saw in that magazine. Perhaps not. I have no way of knowing.

My next exposure to pornography was three years later when we lived in Texas. I was nine, going into the fourth grade. We had moved to Texas to live with my grandparents while my dad was away serving overseas.

One day I was standing at the end of the driveway kicking rocks, waiting for the school bus to come. I saw a scrap of wrinkled paper on the ground. Curious, I picked it up and smoothed it out. It was a bit like a puzzle piece so I tried to figure it out. The piece contained enough graphic imagery that I understood it was a naked man and woman locked in a pose of some sort. I shoved the wadded up picture into my pocket and threw it in the trash can when I got to school.

When we moved again after Dad got back from overseas, this time to California, I was in fifth grade. We lived there three years and my exposure to pornography skyrocketed.

We lived close enough to my school that I could walk. I'd head down the street to cut through the woods to the upper field of the school. One day in those woods I found a whole stack of pornographic magazines that someone had left there. And so a pattern began. I'd sit in the woods and thumb through them. My curiosity growing.

About that same time, we started health classes at school where I received more explanation about the male and female body and sex. The school district felt we were old enough to hear this information so I thought maybe all boys were as curious as me. But in my mind, I doubted that. I'm not sure why.

Now I had the medical explanation for anatomical parts and sex, but I was curious why someone would show their "private parts" for a magazine.

During that time, there were a couple of instances where I actually found discarded pornographic magazines. Some in the woods, along the road, or old, discarded ones in newsstands. Sometimes after swimming at the pool, I'd walk over to a nearby store to look at the popular Mad® magazine[1]. Teen magazines were in the rack, but of course, there were other magazines there too—wide open. I'd look around to see if anyone was looking, thumb through one or two, and then put them back.

The curiosity continued to grow.

Some of my friends told me they found a "dirty" magazine in the woods and tore it up and threw it away. This group of friends I knew didn't go to church, I don't even think they believed in God, but here they were talking about destroying the images while I sat and enjoyed them. I remember thinking, "When I found one of those magazines I didn't tear it up and throw it away. I'm supposed to be a Christian. What's the problem with me? What's going on?"

I remember thinking something was wrong. I began to wonder why I was so curious about such things. But I didn't know what to do about it. Because I was afraid to appear foolish, I didn't ask a lot of questions that might reveal how little I knew.

Shame set in.

There were other instances that fueled my curiosity. After Sunday School at the chapel, which was an ancient building filled with lots of room to explore, we'd roam down all the hallways to see what there was to see. In some of the more removed parts of the building, the bathrooms had graffiti all over the walls including dirty comments and crude drawings of females. As a budding teenager, I didn't know what it all meant.

In an attempt to understand what I saw, I asked my folks about it. Their response was, "You can't keep the birds from flying over your head, but you can sure keep them from building a nest in your hair."

I've heard this expression since then and as an adult I know it means, "Some stuff is going to be around you in life, but you have control over what settles down and makes a home in your mind or what you don't allow."

However, I didn't know what it meant as a kid. The answer didn't help me, but I didn't want to say anything because I felt insecure. I definitely didn't want to look stupid or ignorant, so I didn't ask any follow up questions. Plus, I knew I had no plans to let birds live on my head.

After a while, I began to wonder if I was a magnet to these types of magazines. It seemed like I saw one everywhere I went.

For instance, one summer I flew to another state all by myself to attend camp. This camp was located on a big lake with lots of activities. As I flew up to the town near the camp, my excitement built. This was going to be so fun. I was on my own adventure.

A friend of our family met me at the town's small airport. Cool mountain breezes greeted me as we left the airport to head to their home for the night. The next day I'd head off to camp. I couldn't wait to get there.

Though the drive wasn't too long, I remember looking around as we headed away from the airport. Pulling off the highway toward their home, our family friend stopped at a stoplight. I looked out the window and there on the sidewalk was a dirty magazine—wide open! I couldn't believe it.

Being small and skinny, throughout school and even at that camp, I was picked on quite a bit.

Being bullied hurts. And when I hurt I wanted to stop hurting so I would find ways to feel better. I don't think the pornography was a "medication" at that point, but I did feel good and excited when I saw the pornography.

I didn't understand the direct connection at the time. I now know the "excitement" I felt was the rush of adrenaline and chemical wash in the brain. As Sam Black, writes in *The Porn Circuit*,

> "Porn is exciting...Mix in the anxiety and excitement of using the forbidden, the fear of being caught, and even secrecy, and the brain learns even faster during these intense emotional bursts. With each repetition the brain receives powerful cocktails of signals and hormones that ensure future cravings..."[2]

We all know a teenager does not need any more hormones rushing around their brain. And a "powerful cocktail of signals" has no business in the hands, or rather mind, of a teen. But my adolescent brain was drinking it all in.

# When There's Nowhere To Hide

*Do not be far from me, for trouble is near and*
*there is no one to help.*

Psalm 22:11

## Dave

Our family took a trip to Hawaii during my middle school years. As everyone does in Hawaii, we enjoyed the beach. But the enjoyment ceased when this sunburnt, overweight guy, wearing an ugly Hawaiian shirt, ran past us toward the water with his camera. His labored jog towards the waves caught our attention, but that attention soon landed on a girl wearing no clothes.

There we were on a public beach with a skinny-dipping girl walking out of the water stark naked. I was both shocked and excited. It wasn't something I saw everyday on the beach. The guy kept taking pictures. The girl kept walking up the beach.

23

I remember thinking, "What is going on? She's just walking out of the water with no clothes on! Does she see that guy taking her picture? Doesn't she mind? What is he going to do with those photos?"

Before my freshman year of high school, we moved across the country. By this time, I understood the purpose of sex, but I kept thinking, "Why are people doing this? What is causing them to do this? What would possess someone to put it in picture form and display it for everyone?" Those questions seemed hooked in my brain, routinely tumbling around in my mind.

Once during our time at the base, the family that lived next door asked me to collect their mail while they were gone. The husband received regular issues of Playboy. So, for the next few months, I took advantage of the situation and looked through and read the couple issues that arrived. This access to pornography was too easy. It was there in my hands. It was free and I had an empty house where I could sit and enjoy it.

The dissonance of being a Christian and yet enjoying this stuff became more and more problematic.

For my last two years of high school I chose to go to a boarding high school. My family was moving again—this time to Hawaii. I begged my parents not make me move with them. It did not sound like paradise to me.

I laid out my arguments: I'd be in the minority on the island, a Haole, and the schools weren't as academically rigorous as this boarding school.

Honestly, my real motivation was to get away from the house rules. I figured boarding school would give me freedoms I didn't enjoy at home. Well, the joke was on me. I went from "rules" to "RULES". The good news? I experienced freedom from pornography during those two years because of the school's rigid regulations and busy schedule.

However, my fascination remained.

When I went off to college, pornography was much more available. I remember intentionally fighting the urge to look at anything.

Because I was more aware of the need for purity, I knew my thoughts and desires for the pornography were not pure. Attending a private Christian college meant many of my classes centered around the Bible. There were also expected standards of conduct designed to encourage purity in your mind and body.

There were some times on my trips from college to home and back, I remember fighting the attraction and ease of access to pornographic magazines in airports where it was available on the newsstands.

Part of our academic requirements was participating in weekly volunteer opportunities. During my junior year, I was on a team that led a "release-time class". Release-time is a religious class usually held in mid-afternoon at a local church. Schools often dismissed children early to attend this class. After one class, the other volunteer and I were waiting for the bus at a stop next to a drug store. As I turned around, there in the window was a magazine blatantly displaying a naked woman. I turned away and tried to fight the fascination.

I don't know if everyone experienced the same exposure to pornography, I never talked to anyone about it, but because of my sensitivity it seemed like it was always there. Or maybe it was that Satan knew my weakness and was always putting it in front of me.

# When It's Not So Happily Ever After

*Therefore what God has joined together, let no one separate.*

*Mark 10:9*

## Dave

Kirsten and I met my first week of college. Our paths crossed several times a week as we had a class together. I sat behind her and would tease her quite often. I loved how she came right back at me during those times. It was pretty hard to get her riled up. But it was sure fun to try. As we got to know each other, we discovered we enjoyed each other's company. We'd meet for lunch or dinner before our evening class. She was easy to talk with and fun to be around.

We started dating that spring. By that time, we had many friends in common. Many of our dates involved time with these friends or walks on the beach or exploring the city around the college. Because we were "poor college kids" we didn't go to places that cost a lot of money. Most of the time we walked and talked about our dreams and the things we believed God wanted for our lives. I grew to deeply love her.

The summer between my junior and senior year, I knew I wanted to marry this woman. Kirsten had graduated in May and moved back to her hometown 10 hours away. Already the distance was painful. I knew she was the one for me and I also knew I didn't want to spend any more days than I had to away from her side.

But I made good use of our time apart and worked extra hours at my job to save up enough money to purchase her engagement ring.

I'll never forget the day I picked it up from the jeweler—I was so nervous walking on the city streets. "What if someone noticed the ring box bulge in my pocket and I was robbed?" But I made it safely to my dorm room and hid it in one of my drawers. Periodically, though, I'd pull it out to look at it, anxious for the time I planned to propose. Christmas couldn't come fast enough.

We met at my family home to celebrate Christmas. Seemed like we had so much catching up to do, but I was eager to pop the question I'd been contemplating for months. Finally, while walking together during a velvety snowfall, I proposed and she said, "Yes!" I was ecstatic.

We decided to get married in six months, a week after I would graduate from college.

One week before our wedding, Kirsten flew into town for my graduation. My parents drove my car to graduation. Then Kirsten and I headed to her hometown for the last few days before our wedding. This was it. Our wedding day had finally arrived.

After we were first married, pornography really wasn't an issue. We were busy establishing our new home. I was adjusting to working full-time, being a husband, and learning our way around a new place. Learning to live together in marriage was exciting enough. And I grew to love Kirsten more each day. I thought pornography would no longer be an issue because I was completely satisfied in my marriage.

Unfortunately, after Kirsten and I moved across country for my new job, the internet was almost everywhere virtually overnight. This technology, that now made it easier to do research for my job and communicate with friends all over the world, also made it easier to access questionable images. The internet changed the world and my life.

I was still trying to fight what I know now was a pornography addiction. I would tell myself I shouldn't be looking at these images. But that curiosity was there. I was preoccupied wondering why would people be doing this?

Then my initial fascination changed into wondering what else people were doing. And down the rabbit hole I went. "How could I love my wife as deeply as I did and still be attracted to pornography?"

The possible access to almost anything, by anyone, from anywhere in the world turned my simmering addiction up to a boil.

Before access to the internet, even though I was fascinated by pornography, I'm not sure I was addicted. Viewing pornography in a public place was never an option. When pornography became easily accessible via the internet, that's when it became addictive.

Now I know that there's the rush that goes with pornography, as far as the chemical wash in your brain, the excitement, the high, which trains those neurological pathways to want more.

> "Pornography attachment can be very strong because masturbation and orgasm produce a fireworks display of neurochemicals and repetition builds neural pathways to enable patterns of behavior. The episodes are even more enhanced with other feelings, including fear of getting caught, secrecy, and novelty. This chemical and hormonal explosion takes learning to a whole new level.[1]

One picture leads to another picture leads to another picture creating that constant, hormonal, chemical wash. And then it's like, "Crap! What am I doing? I've been here two or three hours. What am I doing?" Then you sign off the internet and think, "Okay, I'm not going to do that again. That's horrible."

You feel guilt and shame. As high as the momentary thrill was, the low feels even lower.

> "Pornographers want people to believe that viewing porn is harmless entertainment and that it can even spice up one's love life, but the opposite is true. Rather than encouraging intimacy, research shows that porn steals it away.[2]

I would think, "You're working for a Christian ministry. You're supposed to be pure and you're not. You're lousy. It sure sucks being you."

Then I'd decide I was done. I was not going to do that any more.

I'd be successful at this decision for about two to four months.

But a thought would come into my mind or I would see something that would trigger thoughts like, "What about this? What if I did a word search on this? What would I come up with?"

It's amazing how Satan uses innocent thoughts to trap you. I bizarrely discovered you could find questionable images by doing an image search of a random sequence of eight numbers. I found a questionable image one day when I entered a series of numbers on a whim. After that, I was hooked.

I started to see a pattern in these searches which fascinated me. Truthfully, I wasn't just fascinated with seeing patterns; I saw this as a way to hide what I was doing. My thought was if anyone were to see a Google search on such and such numbers it wouldn't raise any red flags.

I was searching this way at work as well as at home.

By this point, finding the images became a game. I would be bored, so I would see what kind of pictures I could find by typing in innocuous things. "I was just messing around," I told myself. Plus, I was safe. There were ways to hide what I was doing even from someone checking my internet search history.

At least that's what I told myself.

However, even though I tried to convince myself that what I was doing wasn't hurting anyone, that I could stop at any time, the reality was very different.

It was at this point that I realized it really wasn't "just a game." Something more was going on. Thus began the vicious shame cycle (see Figure 1):

It felt like I was in a dream trying to run but in super slow motion and not making any forward progress.

This cycle added to feeling worthless, which then fed my feelings of insecurity, which then almost made it feel like it was necessary to feel happy, "medicated" again. And the cycle would repeat and repeat and repeat.

But my "game" came to a sudden end.

# When The Jig Is Up

*You can't whitewash your sins and get by with it;*
*you find mercy by admitting and leaving them.*

*Proverbs 28:13 THE MESSAGE*

## Dave

I had been doing "number searches" at work and someone noticed. I had thought, "There's nothing on here that's going to flag anything so it's not a big deal to do this at work." Even though I knew it was against the corporate policy, I justified my actions because I believed they were untraceable.

I was really careful about clearing the cache (a high-speed storage mechanism on a computer) each time, but I don't think clearing the cache made much difference because they were smarter than that.

*"Secrecy kills; only truth heals."*

*Earl Wilson*

I will never forget when I got the call to go to Human Resources with my supervisor. I remember thinking, "I have a feeling I know what this is about."

And then the panic set in.

I walked into the room and saw the Human Resources representative, the head of Information Technology, and my immediate supervisor.

They informed me they'd been tracking some stuff and set down a stack of papers for me to see what they'd been tracking.

I didn't need to look at the papers because I knew what was on them. I knew I'd been caught red-handed. I had to come clean.

That's when I admitted my struggle with pornography.

They said, "Well, we have help for employees who are doing that. But because you've gotten caught and did not come to us willingly, then there are other ramifications. You need to think about how you are going to deal with this." They were, obviously, not thrilled.

I can't remember all the words we exchanged, I just remember feeling like I was going to vomit.

I do remember answering some question with a comment that obviously did not suffice.

I remember thinking, "Okay now wait a minute. You said there's no right or wrong answer here." But when I gave them an answer, they said, "Well that's not sufficient." I was a bit indignant, hiding behind a false wall to protect my pride.

But when they said, "I don't think you understand the seriousness of this. You need to go home and really think about this. And then tomorrow when we come back together, we want you to have a plan in place concerning what you are going to do."

I knew this was not their problem, it was mine. Heading back to my office, I felt panicked and sick.

*What was I going to do? How had I let this happen? What in the world was I doing?*

I had no idea what they were looking for as far as having a plan in place. Surely I could get this under control.

Or could I?

The remainder of my time at work that day is a blur. I don't recall much of what I did or who I talked with, if anyone. I left work and headed home. My gut in knots.

I'd been caught.

The drive home, normally an enjoyable time to leave work related issues behind, was filled, instead, with anxiety. My job was at risk.

*"What was going to happen?"*

How would I tell Kirsten? I had texted her to let her know I was on my way, but I really didn't want to go home.

*"What would I say?" "How would she react?" "Would she even believe I loved her?"*

Pain seared through my heart. Suddenly, I could see our house. My car crawled into the driveway, carrying my body that felt like lead. *"How did I get here so quickly?"*

That night after dinner, which I couldn't eat, I confessed my pornography addiction to Kirsten. Looking at her face, I knew I'd deeply hurt her. I felt like I was dying, falling over a cliff with no return. We agreed that I had to talk with the kids as well. To my utter astonishment, they immediately forgave me. They saw the real me when I couldn't because of the clutter of lies pulling at my soul.

Kirsten suggested we talk to her co-worker, Cathy, and her husband since they were trained counselors. As she said, we needed immediate help. After meeting with Rick and Cathy, I called my friend, Peter, and confessed my addiction to him as well. I needed help to devise a plan. Thankfully, Peter agreed to meet me for breakfast the next morning.

About midmorning, I was scheduled to meet with my supervisor, the HR representative, and the head of

IT. Same group as the day before. As I wall
the meeting, I felt panic again when I laid
recovery plan Peter had helped me put together.

You could cut the tension in the room with a knife.
All eyes were focused on me. I remember thinking,
*"Will this suffice? Will they accept the plan Peter and
I put together? Will I keep my job?"*

I was almost sick to my stomach during the meet-
ing. If they didn't accept this plan, I had no other
options. I'd be escorted out of the building. My job
immediately terminated. My life felt like it was
ending and it was all my fault. Quietly, I told them I
understood the seriousness of my actions. I laid out
the plan which included counseling, assessment, and
the formation of a Restoration Team—an account-
ability group of 4-6 people. Then I waited and held
my breath for their response.

They accepted the plan. My supervisor was very sup-
portive. Several times during the meeting he indicated
his support of me through his words and actions.
The Human Resources representative expressed
confidence in this plan, along with reiterating how
seriously the organization took pornography addic-
tion. While I could feel the tension in the room, there
was also a sense that each person there wanted me
to succeed.

While I was relieved, I had to put the plan into
action immediately. And they required proof that

I was doing exactly as we discussed. All in all, the meeting didn't last more than 15 to 20 minutes. Although it felt like hours.

They greatly restricted my computer use and access as well as work-related travel. I'd have to send someone else from the department in my place. As the supervisor, I had already been cross-training others in the department to cover the travel for various events. During the next six months, I'd have to remove myself from the schedule except for a couple of pre-approved events.

This was my opportunity to make the personal changes I needed and to keep my job. If I failed to keep my commitment to change my behavior, there wouldn't be another chance.

I called Kirsten to let her know the plan and that it had been approved. She sounded relieved and was so gracious to me when the only thing I could cling to was grace. Then I called Peter to let him know that we definitely wanted to move forward with the Restoration Team under Peter and Debbie's leadership.

# When It's Not Up To You

*In my distress I prayed to the LORD.*

Psalm 118:5 NLT

## Kirsten

I went to work the morning after Dave dropped the bombshell, but was useless.

Physically nauseated. Unable to concentrate. Nerves taut as piano strings.

Dave and Peter were meeting for breakfast. I knew Dave would get Peter's advice on some options to present to his employer. Hopefully these options would meet the company's demands to deal with this pornography addiction and put safeguards in place to keep the addiction from clawing its way back into our lives.

The HR meeting was scheduled for 9:15 a.m.

Cathy suggested we meet at 9:00 a.m. to pray for mercy and God's clear leading. Just as I was getting ready to head for Cathy's office, my phone rang. It was Dave. The HR rep had called him in earlier than planned. My heart pounded so loudly I could hardly hear his next words.

His words, lots of words, seemed to spill out all at once,

"I admitted my addiction to pornography. I laid out some of the ideas we discussed last night with Rick & Cathy and then this morning with Peter. I told them I would see a counselor. They'll pay for the first visit to the counselor, but it has to be within the next week. At this time, I still have a job but I'm on probation for the next six months and not allowed to travel. Peter agreed that we need to get some good marriage counseling. Can we go over to Peter & Debbie's tonight to learn more about the restoration process Peter discussed with me? I think this is something we need to do. I know I've hurt you and that I need help."

I could hear hope in his voice. There was also something else. A pleading, a deep desire for me to not only forgive him but also to believe he was capable of making the necessary change. Keeping his job hinged on the outcome of putting this plan together and walking it out.

While I was relieved and thankful Dave still had his job, I was also reeling from the sharp shift in our marriage. I agreed to go hear about this program that evening. What else could I do?

In a daze, I left my office to meet with Cathy. Tears began afresh as I told her of the phone call. We did pray with thanksgiving for the results of this meeting and for wisdom for the days ahead. We were in uncharted territory. Nothing was certain. Everything was changed.

However, I was dying inside. I just didn't know it yet.

Later that day, Dave made an appointment to meet with a counselor at work. After the initial meeting, the counselor referred Dave to someone more specialized for further counseling.

How I got through that day at work, I don't know. I have no memory of it other than a deep sense of loss.

*"How could he do this? How could he sacrifice our marriage, me, our family, our livelihood, our reputation for something that wasn't real? Why?"*

And I heard, "Because you aren't enough to satisfy him."

# When Friends Believe For You

*The heartfelt counsel of a friend is as sweet
as perfume and incense.*

*Proverbs 27:9 NLT*

That night we drove in silence most of the way to Peter
and Debbie's. Dave glanced over at me often, probably
to see what was going on or to get some sort of response
out of me. We'd spoken only a few words to each other
since we'd left home.

I dreaded this conversation even though I knew Peter and
Debbie were good, trustworthy friends. But how do you
tell people, that might think you have a great marriage, that
your marriage has all been a lie?

Again, I wondered how we got to this place.

I remember walking into their warm home, up the short
flight of stairs, and seeing Debbie at the top. Her first words
to me were, "You can cry all you want."

Unbelievably to me, I began to sob. Who knew you could cry this much?

We followed them to their home office and found chairs. Peter shut the door and began to ask questions. Since Peter and Dave had met earlier in the morning, Peter had a good idea of what had happened. He'd also brought Debbie up to speed.

I sat there. Numb. Angry. Looking at Dave as if to say, *"It's all your fault we are in this situation."* Plenty of judgment and condemnation flowed through my mind and heart. My mind screamed, *"This was all his fault. He really screwed up so he could jolly well figure out how to get us out of this situation."*

Did I mention I was angry?

Peter told us about a proven process that helped married couples who were in trouble. This process from the book, *Restoring the Fallen¹,* centered on a Restoration Team. This Team of four to six people, hand-picked by the couple in crisis, would come alongside the couple and walk this road with them. The goal was to see them fully restored in their marriage, jobs, family relationships, and ministry. It was an intensive process that involved a huge time commitment—18 months to three years—from each Team member. But, Peter had seen great success with this program and had just participated on such a team.

Listening to him describe this, I thought, *"Who do we know that would be willing to invest hundreds of hours to do this for us?"* Just the thought of asking anyone over-whelmed me.

Peter and Debbie then volunteered to be on this Team, if we wanted them to be. They also agreed to lead it. We would have to choose two to four other people on whom we both agreed. And, we would have to personally talk with each person and explain to them the time commitment and reason we desperately needed this Team. A humbling, daunting task.

Peter was confident this Restoration Team process would address Dave's addiction and put accountability in place. This was the plan Dave's employer accepted this morning.

I sat there numb. Quiet. Not offering much unless spoken to directly.

They asked, "Kirsten, what do you think of this plan?" I replied something along the lines that it was better than anything I could come up with, so why not give it a try.

I was so hurt and angry. It was difficult to trust anyone or anything.

I still couldn't believe we were in this situation. Yet, we were.

My attitude was getting worse by the minute.

# When They "Get You" Before You Get You

*Let the redeemed of the LORD tell their story.*

*Psalm 107:2*

The next few nights, Dave and I discussed several peo-
ple to ask to be part of this Restoration Team. We'd
agreed on a Team of six people. Peter and Debbie gathered
the necessary materials to give to each Team member. They
also prayed for us and with us. However, the task of picking
the Team fell to us. And, we had to agree on each person.

No small task.

A few days later, we called some friends from church that
we hadn't known for that long, and asked if we could come
over. Dave worked with Ken as a volunteer at church, and
Jackie and I had been in Bible studies together. We enjoyed
them both, but I wouldn't say our friendship was all that
strong at that point. Our friendship had been developing
over the last couple of years. Plus, our kids were friends,
which gave us more common ground.

Dave and I both felt they could be trusted and would give us wise counsel as part of the Restoration Team.

There are times in your life when you have to admit that God has gone before you. This was one of those times.

When I called, Jackie knew something was up immediately. Since we didn't make it a regular habit of popping over to visit, our request to come see them was a bit unusual. But they didn't hesitate at all when we, basically, invited ourselves over to their house.

They'd been doing some yard work, prior to our arrival, so we joined them on their deck, and admired the newly planted flowers.

It felt awkward at best. We knew why we were there and dreaded this conversation.

Throughout the small talk, I noticed Jackie watched me with a puzzled look. I knew she sensed my discomfort. I felt like I was babbling, talking to cover up my embarrassment.

When they asked, "So how's it going?" Dave told them what had happened and described the Restoration Team to them both.

As he described our need, I felt myself cringe thinking, *"How could we ask this couple we don't know that well to give us eighteen months to three years of concentrated time? They were so busy already. They had a life of their own. Could we really trust them?"*

How I hated and deeply resented this.

Before Dave was even finished explaining the details, Ken and Jackie both interrupted and said, "Absolutely." We were stunned and relieved.

Unknown to us, Ken and Jackie briefly described their struggle. They knew what it was to fight for a covenant marriage. They knew how it felt to be so angry you don't even want to be around the other person. They got it. And they were willing to help.

They assured us we would not only survive, but would also grow from this experience. As they related pieces of their story, we heard hope. We heard how another couple had helped them walk through their struggle.

We left their place relieved. But we still needed one or two more. And we couldn't agree on those people.

I felt sick as I crawled further into the darkness.

# When You Make The Team You Don't Want

*A good friend will always tell you what you need to hear, not always what you want to hear.*

Brady Boyd

Ironically the last two people we asked to be on the Restoration Team were the very first couple we called about Dave's addiction, Rick and Cathy. I approached Cathy at work with the request to join our Team. As counselors, they were familiar with the team concept and were interested in participating. They were wonderful, calm people that I felt very comfortable with because I'd worked with both of them in various capacities for several years. Dave wasn't as familiar with them but felt comfortable with them on our Team.

Rick and Cathy brought another level of expertise to our Team as well as a relentless pursuit of complete honesty, something we would learn we desperately needed.

We would soon find out that while they were compassionate and caring, they were laser-focused on our total healing.

Because of their counseling backgrounds, they easily saw through any smokescreens we put up and quickly called us on that evasion tactic.

Our Team was set.

We provided all contact information to Peter and Debbie, our Team leaders, to set up the initial meeting.

Our Team met without us for the first one or two times to review the process, discuss the parameters of working with us, and pray. They also had to read the book, *Restoring the Fallen*[1], before our meetings could begin.

Peter and Debbie advised against us reading the book until after the restoration process was complete. Though that sounded strange, they assured us it would make sense as we became more familiar with the process.

Within the next week, our first meeting was scheduled and Peter and Debbie reported back to Dave's employer. They would continue to provide regular progress reports to his employer throughout the restoration process.

We had no idea what to expect and were quite nervous. But, we knew we needed help.

Everything began to move quickly, and yet slowly. I struggled to fully comprehend why we were in this situation.

In many ways, I felt like everyone knew the lie we'd been living. I felt like a pariah, an outcast. I was so afraid that if anyone took the time to really look in my eyes, they would see the guilt, the shame I was trying to hide. While I didn't have a scarlet "A" embroidered on my shirt, it felt like a neon sign flashed "imposter" incessantly above both of us. And once the story came out, I was certain we would be destroyed.

I carefully reinforced my protective walls. I couldn't be discovered. I had to protect myself at all costs.

What I didn't know was the personal toll that cost would demand. I learned soon enough.

# The Choice

# When You Don't Know If You Want To Be Whole

*My heart is wounded within me.*
*Psalm 109:22*

D ave's first meeting with a counselor was set up through his employer. After the initial meeting, the counselor felt it was in Dave's best interest to meet with a counselor outside of the office—a marriage counselor who also dealt with sexual addiction. Dave agreed to an initial meeting with this new counselor.

## Dave

I'll never forget Rob's question to me during our initial meeting, "How much is it worth to you for your wife to be whole and to heal?" At that point, I really hadn't thought much about how my addiction was affecting my wife. It was my issue and I needed to deal with it. However, after hearing Rob's question, I agreed to talk to Kirsten to discover if she thought we both needed to be in counseling together. It was important for my wife to heal. I deeply desired and needed her forgiveness.

I knew I had hurt Kirsten deeply and that tore me up. I felt like she hated me. It was uncomfortable to be with her. Was she just being congenial while loathing me under the surface? I knew it wasn't going to be easy to fix this problem.

## Kirsten

Dave and I had discussed marriage counseling, but Dave adamantly felt that since this was "his issue," we didn't need marriage counseling. It was "his problem," so he'd deal with it. Frankly, I kind of agreed, yet I also wondered if marriage counseling would help. Two of the three couples we'd talked with on our Restoration Team suggested we consider marriage counseling. But, I didn't argue with Dave. His mind was set so I didn't see any point in exerting any more energy than necessary.

By this time in the process, I knew how hurt and angry I was with Dave. I didn't know how to talk about it and with whom. So I didn't.

Dave came home from the initial meeting with Rob looking very puzzled. Evidently, during this session, Rob asked Dave if he thought I was unaffected by his pornography addiction. Dave responded the same way he'd responded to me: it was his problem so he needed to work on it. Rob bluntly told Dave that his pornography usage was as if he'd committed adultery—physical infidelity in our marriage.

Dave had never made that connection before that moment. Rob challenged Dave to ask me directly if that was how I felt.

Rob was right. That was how I was feeling, but I hadn't been able to frame the words so succinctly.

I felt betrayed in every area of my life. I felt worthless, unseen, and unlovable. I felt thrown-away. My inner condemning voices were gaining strength every day. And I was losing the battle faster than I realized.

> I felt worthless, unseen, and unlovable. I felt thrown-away.

The dark hole widened its gaping mouth as it sucked me closer to its vortex.

That night Dave looked at me, honestly looked at me, and asked, "Do you think we need marriage counseling?"

Quietly I answered, "Yes, I think it would help. I'm very hurt and angry and confused right now. I feel like our 25 years of marriage have been a sham—like I don't know you."

What I didn't realize at the time was I didn't know me either. Our marriage, though not a total sham, was teetering on the edge of disaster. I sensed it would only take one tiny movement to topple us.

A week later, Dave and I met with Rob, the marriage counselor, together. He surprised me. He wasn't at all what I pictured as a marriage counselor. Of course, I don't really know what I was picturing. But, he took me completely off guard.

Rob's office was located in the same building as a professional group with whom we worked. But his waiting room was in the general foyer that everyone used which made me very nervous. I was so afraid that someone we knew would come out and see us. Then they'd ask a bunch of questions and we'd be discovered.

Shame and embarrassment flooded over me. We were there for marriage counseling and I didn't like it. My false mask of a "wonderful marriage" was ripped off. We didn't have a wonderful marriage. Okay, so now I knew it. But, I wasn't ready for the world to know it.

After talking with Rob for the allotted time, he recommended we do a one-week intensive counseling session. This was four hours a day for five days with daily homework. Rob told us we needed to take "a vacation" from our jobs and totally clear our schedules—I thought, *"Yeah, right, sounds like a trip to the spa."* This would be all-consuming.

I wasn't looking forward to this at all. But, in my mind, I thought this would be "good for Dave" so I'd go through with it.

Funny how we can trick ourselves into believing we are guiltless. Our mind says,

"It's all his fault."

"We wouldn't be in this condition if you didn't...."

"I'll be happy when you...."

And I climbed farther back into the dark cell of the prison.

# When It Starts
# With Commitment

*If someone falls into sin, forgivingly restore him.*
*Galatians 6:1 THE MESSAGE*

The whole purpose for the Restoration Team, called a Spiritual Care team in the book, *Restoring the Fallen,* was to guide the person through authentic repentance to all possible forms of restoration. Part of this process also includes assisting the spouse and family with their needs during this process.

Because the entire process is meant to bring about the person(s) complete restoration to life and ministry, the process typically takes a minimum of eighteen months to three years or more. Also, the team agrees to provide ongoing care as needed.

**Six Purposes of a Restoration Team:**

1. **Spiritual Health.** It is a team of people committed to providing care for a wounded member of the body of Christ...interested in ferreting out the spiritual roots of the problem. The [Team] is also interested in helping the individual come to a place of spiritual health.

2. **Body Life.** The [Team] brings together different spiritual gifts that, when combined, can unleash God's love and power to the [person being restored].

3. **Accountability and sensitivity.** The [Team] acts as an advocate for the spouse or family members who have also been injured...The [Team] holds the sinner accountable to correct harmful patterns toward family members and others in order to rebuild relationships with them.

4. **Penetrating denial and clarifying reality.** Often the one who has fallen into sin is a powerful person who is able to intimidate those around him or her and convincingly present a distorted view of reality, seeking to impose it on others...A spouse or family member who might otherwise be too wounded, confused or insecure to stand alone will benefit from the strength and support of the team.

5. **Synergy.** It is an awesome responsibility to have someone voluntarily put himself or herself under your care for a period of time, so the combined wisdom and consensus of the group, led by the Spirit of God, is very important.

6. **Intercession.** The [Team] is committed to interceding on behalf of the [one being restored], the family and those who fall within the sphere of the person's influence. Praying for God's mercy, strength and restoration is probably the most critical function of the team.[1]
[Bracketed content mine]

"An effective restoration process must deal not only with the ruin of the disaster, but also with the internal, pre-existing weaknesses that caused it...The ministry of restoration involves encouraging a fallen saint to return to fellowship with God and with God's family. Returning is possible because the blood of Jesus Christ cleanses us from all sins[2] and because God extends his mercy to us so that we can return to him."[3]

Galatians 6:1 says, "Brothers and sisters, if someone is caught in a sin, you who live by the Spirit should restore that person gently. But watch yourselves, or you also may be tempted."

This is a biblical approach to restoration and has proven to be very effective.

## Dave

The Team wasn't letting either one of us add to the distance between us. I had to work to communicate with Kirsten on a deeper level. But with the rift between us, this was very hard.

I knew the marriage needed to be mended and I was willing to do whatever it took to make it whole. I loved my wife and I was committed to the marriage covenant even though I'd broken that covenant.

Early on, I asked Kirsten if she was going to leave me. When she answered, "No," (to my relief) I believed her and committed to doing whatever needed to be done to restore our relationship.

# When You Realize Commitment Means You Have No Control

*How can we be loved if we are always in hiding?*

Donald Miller

Our first meeting with the Restoration Team was awkward.

Here were six people we knew well and some quite well. Yet, it felt like walking into a courtroom filled with strangers. We were guilty—well, Dave was guilty, as I still maintained—I was the injured party.

We had no idea what to expect. We trusted Peter and Debbie, yet we were apprehensive.

The Team had met a few days previously to get to know each other, pray, and discuss the parameters of this restoration effort.

Our awkwardness was palpable. Among friends, and yet we felt completely out of place. I was angry and self-righteous. After all, it's not like this was my idea. This was all Dave's fault. I felt justified in my anger and I wore my snotty attitude like a jeweled mink stole.

We sat down to begin the process. I felt sick. My hands shook the entire meeting. I cried. I was embarrassed. I was ashamed to be there.

The Team asked tough questions, painful questions. Deep in my soul I was trying to believe this would all be worth it.

Peter and Debbie went over the particulars for this Team. Then they asked us a question that would change our lives, "Are we an accountability group or an advisory group?"

I was bewildered. *"What was the difference? Isn't that just semantics?"*

Peter went on to explain that an advisory group would give us recommendations about various issues but we could view their opinions as just that—opinions—and we wouldn't meet as often.

However, if they were an accountability group, everything in our life would come under their inspection and jurisdiction. We would not make any decisions without consulting them first. If they decided we shouldn't be involved in something, we wouldn't be involved in it. If they thought we needed to do something, then we had to do it. Basically, they would commandeer our lives for the foreseeable future.

Dave and I looked at each other. This was not an easy decision. Yet, we knew the one we needed to make and it was terrifying.

We were in our mid-forties and we were turning over complete control of our lives to six other people. People we knew, but could we trust them that much? What was our other choice? Talk about out of control! We had to make serious changes, but it was a daunting decision.

We finally decided they would be an accountability group. In total control.

It was the best decision we could have made.

We would meet weekly for the next couple of months. The schedule was laid out. The Team would report regularly to Dave's employer who needed proof he was fulfilling the terms of his probation.

One of the first things we discussed with our Team was our volunteer leadership positions at our church. Because of the situation we were in, everyone agreed that we needed to step down from those positions. One of the men agreed to go with Dave to inform the pastor that he was stepping down. Dave also needed to let the senior pastor know he was removing himself from leadership and why. While I knew both these conversations were necessary, and even right, it was humiliating.

At the time, I was on staff at the same church. These were people I worked with. Now they would be privy to our failures. *"Would the humiliation never end?"* I thought I should resign. After all, what kind of example was I setting? My marriage was in crisis. The voices in my mind slithered their slimy lies around my ears and my heart.

*"Everyone is going to know about you."*
*"When they look at you, they'll pity you."*
*"How can you be trusted?"*
*"Failure."*
*"Loser."*

And on and on they slithered and lied and tormented.

To my huge surprise, the Team decided I should stay on in this role. I thought I was now disqualified from serving on a church staff. The Team didn't agree. My ability to perform my job was not in question.

The Team then discussed our need for marriage counseling. We informed them that we had met with a marriage counselor who recommended we go through an intensive week-long counseling session. However, we weren't sure we needed it. The Team asked a few more questions about the intensive and then decided unanimously that it was the best option for us. And they encouraged us to schedule it as quickly as possible as they believed it was critical to our marriage restoration. Plus, they wanted to know if we had any personality issues, such as narcissism or bipolar disorder that would impact the restoration process. We agreed to contact the counselor, schedule our first meeting, and take the personality assessments.

With each question and decision, I shrunk a little more into the darkness. Drifting more into disbelief over our situation, I struggled to stay focused on my surroundings and the current conversation. Even though I was surrounded by others, I felt completely alone. My sense of loss gouged jagged wounds in my heart.

Dave appeared calm during the meeting. Resigned to the steps we needed to take.

I later learned he was anything but calm. He was scared, confused, embarrassed, and filled with shame at the position he'd put us in. But the only hope we had was this Team.

The Team asked Dave and me several questions designed to assess where we were individually in this crisis. I just remember there was a lot of frank talk about our reality. And it was horribly uncomfortable.

*"This couldn't be real."*

We left that meeting in a daze. What had we just agreed to?

We were out of our comfort zones. We were broken. We were scared. We were no longer in control of our lives. And we weren't really sure what that meant.

Yet, I was a bit smug. This was Dave's problem, not mine. I clutched that smugness in a futile, childish attempt to maintain control in an untenable situation.

That first meeting was unnerving. Yet, the days and weeks to come would filet us like caught, gutted fish on the riverbank.

Just as a surgeon uses a scalpel to cut out the diseased part of your body, so this Team broke through our defenses one by one, slicing and chopping away our protective instincts. It was painful, artful, compassionate surgery—mentally, emotionally, and spiritually. Removing one diseased piece at a time.

I remember one meeting near the beginning of our time together, where Dave tried to joke about the situation. Very quickly, Rick, Cathy, and the others jumped in to force him to see the seriousness of his addiction and the devastation he had caused. This was no laughing matter. At the time, I thought he was just trying to lighten things up a bit the only way he knew how. However, it wasn't appropriate and the Team let us know.

## Dave

Before this crisis I approached the reading of Scripture very intellectually. But during this time the Psalms became more real and important to me as I realized David was going through some very difficult issues and was crying out to God. My heart was more tender toward God's Word.

Our life was paused. At the decision of the Restoration Team, we stepped away from all outside commitments. And it was necessary. As Rob told me, not only did the pornography abuse me, it abused Kirsten. We needed the time to repair and restore personally, as well as in our marriage.

One of the ways we did this was to spend time together each evening learning to talk openly and honestly. This meant we could ask whatever question we wanted. We had to learn to listen to the other person without interrupting and without layering our predisposed beliefs or interpretations on their answer. I had to face Kirsten's anger and pain.

## Kirsten

There was nothing easy about this process. As the days became weeks that turned into months, we learned to truly trust this group of faithful, loving people.

> "... It is critical during the recovery process for both partners to develop close, same-sex relationships to supplement the marriage relationship. Those outside relationships can provide much of the nurturance, empathy, mutual support, and affirmation that both individuals need."[1]

11/19/22 Lord, please provide these and all we need.

Our Team provided these safe, same-sex relationships we needed.

It didn't take long for my sins to surface. While we were in this situation initially because of Dave's pornography addiction, the Team accurately honed in on my sin. Their questions became more pointed, more probing, and more challenging. They confronted my beliefs, attitudes, and actions. And as they did, I saw that they truly accepted me and weren't judging me, therefore it was safe to reveal my pain.

The cracks in my masks were widening. I could see through the bars, yet, my prison door remained locked.

# When You Start
# To Wonder If You Can
# Do Anything Right

*Develop the habit of letting small bad things happen.
If you don't you'll never find time for the life-changing
big things.*

Tim Ferris

About four weeks into the restoration process, I had my employee review. It was the first formal one in several years.

During this review, after getting my feedback on how I thought I was doing and what I could improve upon, my boss informed me that he was "very disappointed" in my work. "In fact," he said, "we can't continue like this."

Shocked, I asked several questions to get a better sense of his disappointment. However, my last question was the most important one in my mind, "Do you want me to continue as your assistant?"

He answered, "I don't know."

My tenuous control started to slip. I left the meeting and walked to the restroom as the tears began to flow.

Another failure.

How could this be? There'd been no warning. In fact, from what I remember, it had been quite the opposite. All I'd heard over the last few years had been how thankful he was for me, how hard I worked, and how amazed he was at how much I accomplished.

My world was crumbling around me. My protective wall was collapsing.

I pulled myself together and headed back to my office to complete the remainder of the tasks to get done before the weekend. Turning off my mind and emotions, I kicked into autopilot to get everything done, glancing frequently at the clock counting the seconds until I could leave.

While standing at the copier to complete my last task before the weekend, a friend of mine walked in and noticed, I believe, my red eyes. I'm an ugly crier so it's pretty hard to hide.

Her simple, heartfelt question, "Are you okay?" almost pulled the last brick from my collapsing wall.

"No," I answered honestly, "but I will be." I lied again. I lied to protect my wounded heart and pride.

I wasn't okay. I was shattered. I failed. Again.

The voices menacingly whispered, *"See you aren't good enough. Failure. Unwanted. Not talented enough to keep this job. Worthless."*

I finished the project, thankful that by now everyone else had left. I closed my office and turned off the light to match the growing darkness inside of me.

As I drove home, the voices got louder, screaming venomous accusations and pouring acid into my wounds. My tears, barely contained at the office, now flooded so furiously I could hardly see the road. How I got home safely I do not know, but, by the grace of God, and I'm sure a few wounded guardian angels along the way, I did.

When Dave got home that night, I told him about my review. And I crawled farther into the darkness. My crumbling wounded spirit believing the lies from those voices.

Dave suggested I call the women on our Restoration Team and talk it through with them.

The next morning, curled into the corner of our couch in a fetal-like position, I proceeded to call each of the women and tell them what had happened. I honestly don't remember all their responses, other than their promise to pray and willingness to meet with me if I wanted. I turned them all down. I had already decided that I couldn't stay in this job. One of the women suggested that I go in on Monday and ask my boss specifically what he wanted me to change. I told her I couldn't do that, because by saying he didn't know if he wanted me to stay on, he had, in effect, fired me. I would turn in my resignation first thing Monday morning and clear out my office. There was no reason to stay.

I know now that my physical and emotional reaction was that of a person suffering from PTSD (Post-Traumatic Stress Disorder). I was traumatized; therefore, my "fight or flight mechanism triggered" and I ran.

Monday morning came. I was there early, already packing up a few less noticeable things in my office. My boss arrived and I requested a meeting with him and our Human Resources Director where I presented my written resignation effective immediately. I left the meeting and went back to my office to pack up.

In a few minutes, my boss entered my office and closed the door. He was stunned. He asked if I would stay. If there was anything that would change my mind. He asked why I was leaving. I told him, "Because when I asked you if you wanted me to stay, you said you didn't know. That told me you didn't want me here."

He then asked if I would work a couple of hours a day over the next two weeks to train others to cover for me. And, would I put together a list of all the things I did.

Though it felt ironic, I agreed to put together the list and get it to him in the next couple of days. And, yes, I would come in and train others on a few, key tasks.

Other than that, I needed to begin searching for another job. After all, Dave's job situation was precarious, so I knew I needed a job.

And I left.

Miraculously, within three weeks, I had a new job. It was a contract job for another international business in a nearby city.

By this time, we had decided we would definitely do the intensive marriage counseling, so one of the first conversations I had with my new boss was to inform them I needed an entire week off within the first month of starting my new job. When asked why, I honestly explained that my husband and I were going through intensive marriage counseling because our marriage was in trouble. And thankfully, she understood. God had placed me in a job with a boss who was sensitive and understanding. I was granted the week off without hesitation.

I didn't know the bombshell was only weeks ahead.

# When You Have To Decide If You Do Or You Don't

*You spread out our sins before you—our secret sins—*
*and you see them all.*

*Psalm 90:8 NLT*

I felt perfectly right in my anger, pain, and angst. After all, I was the wronged party.

I'd honored and kept all my vows. He hadn't. He'd traded reality for an image. How could he? Every time it came to mind the pain of this betrayal poured gasoline on my burning anger.

*"How could he?"*
*"How could I stay with him?"*
*"Do I have a choice? Or, being the 'good Christian girl,' do I have to stick this out?"*
*"Do I want to stay or leave?"*

Yet I was haunted by one question.

"Was I a liar?"

*"I told God, in front of everyone, that I would love, honor, and commit my life to Dave until I died. Did I mean it? Or was I a liar?"*

I couldn't get this question out of my mind.

*"But, Dave is the one who's addicted to pornography! He's the one who traded me for some plastic, Photoshopped® image. He's the one who's taken our marriage vows and trampled on them!"*

All the justification and excuses didn't silence that voice. The question wouldn't leave me and then another question joined the choir, "Is God big enough to get you through this and save your marriage?"

This was my choice. MY choice.

> The question wouldn't leave me, "Is God big enough to get you through this and save your marriage?"

One evening not long into our Restoration Team meetings, Dave and I were sitting in the living room, working through some questions from the Team. I believe the lessons were on honesty. Obviously, up until this time, we hadn't been totally honest with each other. Now, what did we have to lose? Our lives were a wreck.

With a pain-filled voice, Dave once again asked if I was going to leave him.

Rather quickly, I said, "No," but my heart rebelled because I wasn't entirely truthful, though I hated the thought of divorce. And because of that, I wanted us to survive at some level. But I tasted that answer in my throat, almost choking on it. My sense of justice reared its head demanding payment. I wanted to scream, "Do you feel this? I want you to feel like this. Feel this pain. I want payment for my pain."

I was wronged.
I was abandoned.
I was hurt.

I. I. I. Me. Me. Me.

In the middle of my internal tantrum, I felt a quiet rebuke, almost like a soft tap on my shoulder. An "ahem." A not-so-subtle signal from the Lord that I needed to stop my ranting and raving long enough to listen.

It wasn't what I wanted to hear at the moment. I wanted agreement that I had every right to retribution. Dave had sinned. God didn't like sin, right? I was in pain. I didn't want to be reminded of my marriage vows. And yet the Lord patiently prompted me again to stop my ranting long enough to hear what He had to say. My guilty conscience betrayed me once more.

Reluctantly, with arms folded and jaw set (think of a pre-schooler's temper tantrum scowl), the Lord began to unfold my arms and heart, and break through. The Holy Spirit began to remind me of my own words.

*I, Kirsten, take you, David, to be my lawfully wedded husband, to have and to hold from this day forward, for better for worse, for richer for poorer, in sickness and in health, to love, cherish, and to obey, forsaking all others and keeping myself only unto you, till death us do part, according to God's holy ordinance, in the presence of God I make this vow.*

## "From this day forward."

There's a starting point, but there's no caveat. I didn't say in my vows, "Starting today—as long as I'm happy."

I didn't say, "Today I'm going to be your wife, but if I become disenchanted with you because you aren't who I thought you were, all bets are off."

God, the Father, began to challenge me with my own words. My vow. I'd started this journey 25 years ago. I'd agreed that I would stick it out no matter what.

*Did I mean it?*

## "For better for worse."

If I was honest, things had mostly been "better." Yes, we'd had those times that were "worse," yet I can't say our marriage was terrible. I'd always felt incredibly blessed by my husband. Up until this point.

Quietly and gently, the Father brought memories of all the good, the "better" we'd lived. Beautiful, sweet memories I couldn't, no, *didn't* want to forget.

Yet, this definitely wasn't good. It didn't "feel" good. "But," the Father asked, "*Did you mean what you said?*"

I couldn't answer.

## "For richer for poorer."

Well, we definitely weren't rich, but we'd always had what we needed, and then some. Dave worked very hard to provide for me and our family. I couldn't disagree on this one. I had no complaints.

*I meant this one.*

## "In sickness and in health."

Okay, Dave had carried the brunt of this one with all my sicknesses. Throughout our entire marriage, my health had always been an issue. For the entire first decade, I'd struggled with one illness after another for ten months out of every year. In fact, I'd been ill more than I'd been healthy. And Dave was always loving and caring despite the strain this put on our budget and relationship.

Physically I struggled to keep up with this man who had boundless energy. Many times, he would give up a desired activity because I wasn't physically able to do it with him. I longed to be as active as he was, but my wishes and reality were very different. Sure, Dave had illnesses as well, and we all like to chuckle about men being babies when they are sick, but he had been tested often by caring for me during my sicknesses.

Again, the Father asked, "So. *Did you mean it?*"

And I cringed.

I felt myself shrinking from God's piercing gaze as He brought back memory after memory of Dave's faithfulness and care. I wanted to hide from His surgically precise knife operating on my pride and arrogance.

*"Did you mean what you said?"*

## "Forsaking all others."

Yeah, I'd done this! My heart screamed, *"I'm good on this one. I've been completely faithful. He hasn't."*

And I heard a quiet, "Really?"

My pride and arrogance wilted slightly.

My mind recalled the romance books I read that had just enough sexual language to stimulate me. "That response is supposed to be toward your husband *only*," He quietly reminded me. "What about your dreams of another, who isn't your husband, finding you attractive?" I remembered a specific book I'd been reading when I became convicted about the direction the book unfortunately headed. It'd been a great character study with a strong story line up to that point. But I clearly sensed in my conscience the book was dangerous. Call it gut instinct or the voice of the Holy Spirit, I knew that if it wasn't appropriate for me to read the book, it was wrong to give it to another, so I tore it apart and threw it away. The conviction was that strong.

Shannon Ethridge, in Every Woman's Battle, says:

> *"While it is normal and healthy to have fantasies, they need to be restricted to your marriage partner...fantasizing about anyone else is mental and emotional unfaithfulness to your husband."*[1]

I was reminded that if a man looks at a woman with lust[2] in his heart, God calls that adultery.

*Had I kept my mind pure towards my husband? Had I flirted with others in my mind?*

I shrank back not wanting to respond to this pointed question.

My pride and arrogance began to crumble. Another piece cracking off my mask.

Exposed.
Fake.
Dishonest.
Not so innocent after all.

## "Until death us do part."

Hmmmm. This one stopped me cold. Though I felt enough pain I wanted to die, I was very much alive.

Which is why it hurt.

*"Did you mean it?"* God asked me again.

*"But isn't this grounds for the death of our marriage?"* I thought, recalling the Scripture passage that talks about

adultery being grounds for divorce.[2] Pornography was adultery in the mind.

"You've done this, too, remember? We just went over this," the Father said. "So, Dave, has grounds then too. Let me ask you again, 'Did you mean it?'"

## "In the presence of God I make this vow"

The questions continued as the Father reminded me, "You didn't just say it to Dave. **You said it to Me.** Let me rephrase it this way:

> Am I big enough to overcome this hurt, this betrayal, this obstacle?
> Am I strong enough to restore your marriage?
> Or are you going to quit?"

Surprisingly, it had nothing to do with Dave.

**It was my vow.**

*Was I going to keep my word or walk away?*

I had other friends in the same situation who had walked away. They were the "wounded party." I get it. They had been wronged. So had I, right? Yet, the question remained, waiting for my answer.

A memory of one friend popped into my head. She'd been in a similar situation. I recalled how she tenderly told me, after her "perfect" marriage shattered, she began wearing an attractive accessory to remind her how complicit she was in her marriage problems. While her husband had acted on his desire, she confessed she had mentally done the same thing. *She was just as guilty.* If their marriage were to survive, and it did, they both had to grow up and work together.

Best-selling author, Stephen Covey says,

> *"Love is a verb. Reactive people make it a feeling... If our feelings control our actions, it is because we have abdicated our responsibility and empowered them to do so. Proactive people make love a verb. Love is something you do: the sacrifices you make, the giving of self, like a mother bringing a newborn into the world...Love is a value that is actualized through loving actions. Proactive people subordinate feelings to values. Love, the feeling, can be recaptured."*[3]

For the first time since Dave's confession of this addiction, I had to confront more than my hurt and anger.

## I had to confront my vows.

I had to confront my own words and decide if I was telling the truth. Or, would I choose to stand one day before my Lord and Savior and tell Him I was "just kidding, it was too hard to forgive."

After all, God had forgiven me completely of my rebellion and sin. Was I really going to tell him this was too much to forgive?

My marriage was hurting because of sin. My sin and Dave's sin. We both had broken our vows.

Love is a verb. Love is a choice.

This was my choice. My. Choice.

Though this truth was breaking through my hardened heart, I wasn't ready to concede "my rights" yet. My hands flew to my ears to muffle the shattering sound of my rigid defenses.

Until one phone call.

# When You Hear Your Son Say, "Do You Love My Dad?"

*But deal well with me, O Sovereign Lord, for the sake of your own reputation! Rescue me because you are so faithful and good. For I am poor and needy, and my heart is full of pain.*

Psalm 109:21-22

Our youngest son was at school overseas.

Nate was enrolled in school at Tauernhof, in Schladming, Austria. He chose this school because Austria is known for its music culture and snowboarding. Basically, two of his favorite things!

In fact, Nate's school was right at the base of one of the Austrian Ski Team's training runs. Talk about ski in, ski out! A Colorado boy's dream! More importantly, it would give him an opportunity to travel and see Europe, something he'd always wanted to do.

The school only had one phone for student use; therefore, we weren't allowed to call unless it was an emergency. And, while Nate had a cell phone, it didn't have an international calling package. Plus, with the time zone differences and varied schedules, we never really knew when he was available.

We'd sent him a message to call home. Though this felt like an emergency, we decided to wait for him to call us. He'd replied to our email so we knew he would. Finally, about a week later, he called. Dave talked with him and told him what had happened and the steps we were taking. Nate seemed to take it all in stride.

However, a few weeks later, while we were out of town participating in a conference, Nate called me to talk. He obviously had processed the shock a bit more and had questions about how I was doing. I answered as honestly as I could and listened as he talked about what he thought. It was obvious to me he was hurting too and was struggling with being away from home with this crisis going on in our family.

The conversation seemed to wander around quite a bit as I let Nate direct it. Finally, though, we got to the crux of his call. I'll never forget his next words.

"Mom, do you love my dad?"

And he began to cry.

With tears flowing and voice breaking, I answered him honestly, "Nate, I love your dad because I made a promise to God. It's actually about my covenant with God. Right now, though, I don't like him very much. I'm hurt and I'm angry."

Thinking of Nate's question still brings tears to my eyes along with wrenching emotions. Hearing my pain reflected in my youngest child's voice was excruciating. He was thousands of miles away. There was nothing I could do to ease his pain and his fear. My mother's heart broke. I had to trust God to heal Nate's wounds and calm his fears.

In that moment, I realized the answer to his direct question. And for the first time I felt the stirring of hope for our marriage.

I had the answer to the Father's repeated question to me.

"Did you mean what you said?"

We would survive because God WAS *big enough* to get us through this crisis. *Amen*

I would survive because I didn't want to face God one day and tell Him I lied to Him on my wedding day.

Now I had a glimmer of hope.

The light began to penetrate the dark corners of my prison warming and illuminating small parts of my world, though the door remained locked.

# The Community

# When You Discover You Were Never Alone

*O God, listen to my cry! Hear my prayer! From the*
*ends of the earth, I cry to you for help when my*
*heart is overwhelmed. Lead me to the towering rock*
*of safety,*

Psalm 61:1-2 NLT

At the urging of our Restoration Team, we participated in a listening and healing prayer seminar[1]. Neither of us had ever been to something like this. But, we were accountable to our Team and this was something they knew we needed to do. The next seminar in our area was scheduled for early November. We checked our calendars for any work conflicts, blocked off that Saturday, and registered online.

Because I didn't think this was something we needed to do, I went purely out of obedience. As we pulled up to the building, we noticed the other cars. "Great," I thought sarcastically, "there are a lot of people here." After parking in the designated area, we hesitantly walked into the building and found the room already mostly filled.

I felt out of control, totally exposed, and completely jagged emotionally. Dave's expression told me he felt about the same.

Hoping to be invisible, we found two seats at a round table in the back corner. A table for six. A set-up designed to encourage discussion which was that last thing we wanted. We knew no one at this seminar. And we didn't have the emotional capacity to be friendly or seek new friendships. We were there. Just...there.

We were now surrounded by a circle of new acquaintances, many who didn't always speak but some who would say what was on their heart, if they felt able. Neither Dave nor I spoke at all unless we were asked a direct question. Our small talk felt stilted and awkward.

As for me, I preferred to be invisible if possible. So, I listened and wrote as directed by the leader. I wrote down thoughts that came to mind, not totally sure that what I was hearing had anything to do with reality. I was going through the motions with little confidence in the process.

Suddenly, I began to tremble. Since I was surrounded by a room of virtual strangers I desperately struggled to maintain control. But the stress of the thoughts and memories were too difficult. Like a cornered animal, I scanned the room for an escape route.

There were rooms we could go to if we needed help, and I needed it now. I found one of these private rooms and blurted out what I was feeling to the counselor who rose to greet me. Mortified at the tears cascading down my cheeks, a memory from my childhood overwhelmed me.

It was a seemingly silly memory, which made no sense and definitely did not explain my convulsive reaction to it.

After I finished recounting my memory the counselor asked one question that changed forever how I viewed this memory:

"Where is Jesus?"

*"Huh?"*

I didn't know if I understood the question and asked her to clarify.

She said, "In the room, where do you see Jesus? Is He there? What is He doing?"

I closed my eyes and asked Jesus where He was during this incident. This was a totally foreign exercise for me. I wasn't in the habit of listening for or identifying God's voice. At the counselor's urging, I waited. And then I had a clear picture of Him. Arms open wide with sorrow-filled eyes. He was there and He felt my pain.

I sobbed with joy. I wasn't alone in that moment. A moment that had brought me repeated pain for decades. A moment filled with shame and embarrassment. A small, insignificant childhood moment to anyone else, yet I bore the scars and the pain all these years. Shame etched onto my mind. But now, because of Jesus, I realized the truth of that incident. And the shame fled.

It was the first time I experienced Jesus redeeming a shameful memory. For the first time in my life, shame's suffocating stranglehold fell away. I had my first breath of freedom. And it was so sweet.

Later that evening, in the security of our own home, I told Dave about this memory and the resulting freedom I felt after going through the exercise with the counselor. I described the memory, and the questions the counselor walked me through. While Dave was thankful I'd had this experience, he felt a little bewildered by the whole seminar. His experience was nothing like mine, leaving him with more questions than breakthroughs.

# When You Think You
# Have Nothing To Hide

*The LORD will keep you from harm—he will watch
over your life; the LORD will watch over your coming
and going both now and forevermore.*

*Psalm 121:7-8*

At our initial meeting, Rob told us to take the week off from work. Though our counseling was local, he instructed us to treat it like we were out of town. No business calls. No dinner with friends, not that we were in contact with many of our friends these days anyway. No internet usage. We were to clear our schedules from all normal activities. Our employers, children, and Restoration Team knew what we were doing that week, but that was it. Basically, we put our lives in "Do Not Disturb" mode.

By the time we began our intensive week with the counselor, the Monday after Thanksgiving, we'd been meeting with our Restoration Team for three months. While we'd made progress, there was still much we needed to deal with and figure out.

I was still angry, defensive, hurt, and generally in blame mode. Dave was defensive and emotionally needy. We had a long way to go to learn to communicate honestly and effectively.

I remember the first day well. It was cold and kind of gloomy, as if the weather was mimicking how I felt.

By now I knew I wanted our marriage to survive. Though I knew that God was strong enough to get us through this crisis, I was still dealing with my hurt and anger. Our Restoration Team helped us identify several broken areas of our marriage where we needed help and had high hopes for this intensive counseling week.

I was, in fact, very apprehensive.

*"What if this pornography issue revealed a more sinister side to Dave? What else would come out in this counseling that would shred the remaining fragments of my heart? Would we get to the end of this week and find out there really wasn't hope for our marriage like I thought?"*

I was here, but I wanted to be anywhere else.

Nevertheless, I pasted on what I hoped was a pleasant, compliant expression. We sat down on a love seat, which I found ironic, and faced the counselor. Dave reached for my hand. He was nervous, too. I guess he needed the physical assurance. I submitted to his grasp, though I would rather not have held his hand.

Rob explained what would happen during the week. There were some standardized tests we had to complete that night to give him a good idea of what he was dealing with. Our sessions would last four hours every morning. We would have assignments to do in the afternoon. We needed to make sure we got adequate rest each night. He recommended we not watch any television, especially the news. He also assured us we would get into some tough issues, and nothing was off limits. Finally, he told us that he was our counselor—not our friend—and as such he was totally neutral. And, he would be honest about his observations and findings.

Since this counseling was mandated by Dave's employer and our Restoration Team, we signed release forms giving the employer and the Team complete access to the counselor's findings. He would file a report with both at the end of our time. Once again we learned privacy was a luxury we no longer possessed.

And so we began.

The first day we spent going over why we were here along with some of our personal history. Rob surprised me several times by how insightful he was. I'd been fooled by his soft-spoken manner. This guy was no pushover. He began teaching us about how certain visible behaviors are the cover for deeper issues and if all we do is treat those behaviors nothing changes. Rob told us his job was to delve beneath the behavior, to the root cause, so that behavior is changed.

I smugly thought, *"Good. Dave needs to stop this pornography thing if we have any hope of surviving."*

We left at lunchtime with tests in hand along with reminders not to watch television or spend time on the internet. Our drive home was silent.

After a quiet dinner, we both went to separate corners to complete our tests. I found my attention wandering and simply answered the first thing that came to mind. I figured I could make these tests say what I wanted them to say; it was all Dave's problem. I was fine. F.I.N.E.

The next day, our counseling got more intense. Rob asked more disturbing questions about both of us. We discussed our early years, school years, how we met, early marriage— pretty much anything he wanted to ask.

- What was your home of origin like?
- What about your family dynamics?
- When was your first exposure to pornography?
- Why did you believe you had to hide your real emotions?
- Did you recognize any signs of pornography?
- How often do you initiate sexual intimacy?
- How do you express anger?

Often I was uncomfortable with how he probed into the information we provided. And when he began to question my deeply held beliefs, I got a bit miffed. He was starting to shed uncomfortable light on mistaken beliefs (or lies) I clung to firmly.

Like I said, Rob was a smart, intuitive man. He quickly saw through our excuses and pushed to the root of several issues. I was beginning to feel rather uncomfortable and resented the process even more.

We left with another round of "homework." Questions we needed to discuss openly and honestly. Not something I was looking forward to at all. We were both very tired.

But we went home and began the process of working through the questions. I remember feeling defensive, angry, and self-protective. I felt bruised enough. No way was I getting more hurt!

Looking back, I wish I had journaled more about this time. But my journals are surprisingly silent during this week of counseling. In my mind, I'd written stacks and stacks about it. Guess that tells you where my mind was. My memory is very fuzzy at this point.

Until the next day. The day of our diagnoses.

# When You're Pointing A Finger In The Wrong Direction

*My help comes from the LORD, the Maker of heaven and earth. He will not let your foot slip—he who watches over you will not slumber.*

Psalm 121:2-3

Miracles happen every day. But sometimes you're in such a bad place, you simply can't see them.

The day we received our diagnoses was one of those days. It was the day our counselor revealed our psychiatric and personality test results.

Rob started with Dave.

"Well, there's good news. Your results show you have very low self-esteem and self-image. All the indicators show that your pornography addiction is simply your medication of choice for dealing with your low self-image. I don't see any personality disorders or anything like that. We can deal with this. We'll identify your triggers, deal with the root issues related to the self-esteem, and come up with ways to overcome this addiction. It's great news."

I was so relieved. Honestly relieved and hopeful. Dave was too by the look on his face. I saw him relax for the first time in months. I think we both deeply exhaled at the same time.

It was my turn. I wasn't worried. After all, Dave's problem forced us to come here. And now that we knew his addiction was treatable, things might get better.

I smiled as Rob turned to me, but not for long. Gone was his smile and relaxed posture. Suddenly I felt extremely nervous.

He leaned in, looked intently at me, and very seriously said, "I have to ask you a question. Have you recently, or ever, considered taking your own life?"

I felt the room tilt. WHAT?!!!

Shocked, I answered, "No. Never. Why would you ask me that?"

"Your results are serious. In fact, you need medical help immediately. You need to contact your doctor and get on medication in the next couple of days. Otherwise, I have to put you in the hospital."

*"A hospital? Is he talking about putting me in a psyche ward?"* I internally gasped.

*What was he saying? This wasn't about me; it was about Dave. I'M okay. I'M fine. What is he talking about? This. Is. About. Dave.*

I sat there stunned as tears began to slide down my face.

"You have suicidal depression, PTSD (Post-Traumatic Stress Disorder), and moderate anxiety disorder. The suicidal depression is very concerning. You've had this for a while," he said.

*"The tests are wrong,"* I thought. *"I'm not depressed. That's crazy."*

But he wasn't joking. And I began to free-fall into the darkest place of my life.

In the dark I began to think: there had been times in the past when God attempted to get my attention about my state of mind by using a divine 2x4. While I rubbed the imaginary knot on my head and gave nodding assent to what He was trying to teach me (and the depression He was trying to reveal), I never paid close attention.

The Father helped me recall the anxiety attacks that started after the birth of my son.

The first time I experienced an anxiety attack, I thought I was having a heart attack. The pain started in my left side and moved quickly up to my neck followed by difficulty breathing. I felt my heart race like stampeding horses. And then in a few extra-long seconds it was done. I was left with general exhaustion and a sense of doom. That was it. However, the next one hit a few days later with more intensity.

It felt like a huge tsunami wave crested over the top of my head. My breathing quickened and I began to panic. Forcing myself to breathe deeply and slowly, the attack eased. I was totally shaken, and sure I was losing my mind. I had two small children. I couldn't feel like this!

After several more panic attacks, each with increasing intensity, I worked up the courage to mention it to a friend of mine. She immediately recognized the symptoms, as she had suffered with anxiety attacks during postpartum. At least now I was pretty sure I wasn't crazy. She told me to call her when one happened and she would talk me through it. Such a sweet gift.

However, the attacks increased to the point that I finally talked with my doctor about them. He felt my self-diagnosis was spot on and that there was nothing medically to be done. I needed to figure out the root cause and deal with it.

I didn't.

I told myself my son was fine and I just needed to get over the anxiety, applying all the appropriate Christian clichés: God won't give me more than I can handle; just trust the Lord and everything will be fine; perfect love casts out fear; everything happens for a reason; God's got this.

I dealt with the pain by putting a bandage on it. A clumsy dressing of happy, spiritual thoughts. But the wound— the thoughts, the accusations—was still there, festering, spreading its poison through my heart, mind, and body. I just kept applying larger bandages.

But not this time. Not the day of my diagnosis.

This time, God dropped the 2x4 and used a railroad tie. In every way but physically, I was knocked flat. God had my stubborn attention this time.

A myriad of jumbled thoughts ricocheted through my mind.

"Are you okay?" Dave or Rob asked, which one said it I can't recall. Out of stubborn habit, I nodded my head. Who was I kidding! I wasn't all right at all. Another lie. I was descending quickly and frighteningly into blackness. I was swiftly turning totally numb. There was quicksand under my feet. Everything felt unstable. Even my vision dulled.

Sensing my shock, Dave reached for my hand and gave it a squeeze. Out of the corner of my eye, I saw him focused intently on my face. Despite all we'd been through in the last months, he knew me pretty well. His body language and hand pressure let me know he was right there with me. Yet, I felt totally alone.

We took a break shortly after this bombshell. I looked at Dave and mumbled, "Guess I should call the doctor's office huh?" A pitiful attempt at humor. I walked to a back corner of the office suite and dialed the number.

I got through immediately. "I need to make an appointment with the doctor as soon as possible, preferably in the next day or two."

"Well, we just had a cancellation for 1:00 p.m. Can you make that?"

It was 10:30 a.m. Our session was done at 12:30 p.m. Unbelievable. A miracle.

"Yes, I can do that. Thank you."

"What do you need to see the doctor about?" she asked.

I stumbled over the word, "Depression," fighting back the tears but losing the battle. It seemed the tears were no longer under my control, determined to continually pour out of my eyes no matter how hard I tried to pull myself together.

"Okay," she said. "We'll see you at 1:00 p.m. today."

My tenuous emotional grip continued to slip. Stunned, I walked back to tell Dave and Rob about the appointment. Rob was very pleased and surprised that I'd acted so quickly and secured an appointment for that afternoon.

Who gets an appointment these days two and a half hours after you call? This was not usual. It was, in fact, another miracle.

"Before you ask, I have answered[1]," the Father promises.

God knew I needed immediate assistance and had already paved the way.

I don't remember much more of that counseling session. Dave tried to encourage me. Rob tried to encourage me.

I do remember Rob saying that I needed to continue with another counselor who specialized in suicidal depression. But much of it is still very fuzzy.

I was shutting down, crawling into the darkest, lowest part of my self-made prison, yet even that felt strangely insecure. The jailer's door clanged shut behind me as the darkness descended.

# When You're The Last One To Know

*My health may fail, and my spirit may grow weak, but God remains the strength of my heart; he is mine forever.*

Psalm 73:26

We headed to the doctor's office, signed in, and went back to a room surprisingly fast. I looked at the exam table and sat down on the floor, in the corner, with my knees pulled up. Suddenly I was more exhausted than I'd ever been.

Dave sat in the chair watching me with great concern.

The doctor came in and saw me in the corner. Quietly he said, "Tell me what's going on."

I choked out the counselor's diagnosis and Dave filled in the pieces I couldn't remember. The doctor spoke compassionately the whole time. "I've wondered the last couple of times I've seen you," he said. "Some things you've said didn't add up. What tests did you take?"

Dave gave him the information. I signed the necessary forms granting permission to get copies of the test results.

"You're going to be okay," the doctor said. "There are many medication options we can choose from and we'll start at the lowest dose. We'll work on this together to get it right." He was concerned but hopeful.

I wasn't so sure.

I was scared and lost. My mind unsuccessfully trying to process this day's revelations.

*"I'm the one who's sick?! This was all about Dave. This was never supposed to be about me!"*

I railed against the diagnosis, wrestling to understand.

I'd been leveled by a divine railroad tie. Straight to the head and heart. God was serious about dealing with the secret hidden pain I'd harbored all these years. I cowered in the shadows, collapsing on the cold, murky surface. Crumpling against the familiar prison walls.

I was ashamed.

*"How could a 'good Christian' be suicidally depressed?"*
*"How could I not know it?"*
*"Was it possible to believe in God and still be depressed?"*

My heart, mind, emotions, and belief system were ripped open. The putrid sickness spilled out. There was no covering up this infection. No pretending. No hope of repairing the mask. I was exposed as the fraud I was.

The time to deal with me had arrived.

I was very sick. Not Dave. ME.

His pornography addiction provided the impetus for my healing. His crisis was about to save my life.

> His pornography addiction provided the impetus for my healing. His crisis was about to save my life.

My descent into the darkness was sudden and immediate. It felt a lot like Alice going down the rabbit hole with one distinct difference—there was no Wonderland.

The free-fall continued as I slowly shut down.

After we picked up the new medication, I asked Dave if I should inform our Restoration Team. He thought it was a good idea, probably sensing my tenuous hold on reality at that point. After dinner, I called each woman on the Team and told them. Every time I said the word "depression" I slid deeper into the darkness. I don't remember much other than their extreme love and concern.

And curious lack of surprise.

## Dave

Each meeting with the Restoration Team was uncomfortable. I was under the microscope and I hated being in the spotlight. In all honesty, I was rather relieved with Kirsten's depression diagnosis because it took the spotlight off me.

At least temporarily.

I know that sounds horrible, and it is, but believe me when I say, "I know the value of honesty." It's priceless.

# When You Rip Off The Scab

*"Having integrity is about being the same person on the inside that we are on the outside, and if we don't have integrity, life becomes exhausting."*

Donald Miller

My next call was to Mom, my prayer warrior. As I choked out the diagnosis, she shared her concern. But one thing caught her attention—my mention of PTSD. "How do you have that?" she asked bewildered.

I haltingly revealed my secret. "I was sexually abused," I told Mom. "When?" she asked, the sorrow achingly evident in her tone. I described the day to her as delicately as I could.

It was a sunny day, a Saturday, I think. I'd been playing with the kids in our neighborhood in my playhouse, a favorite pastime for my friends and me, not a care in the world. It was afternoon on a beautiful September day. Fall weather would be approaching very soon so I was taking advantage of the warmth by spending as much time outside as possible.

That's when he arrived. I knew him well so I thought nothing of him showing up unexpectedly. He asked if I wanted to go for a bike ride with him. "Sure," I thought and ran to the house to let my grandmother know I was going for a bike ride with him, she knew him too. I told her we would be back very soon.

My parents were away this weekend celebrating their anniversary. Their absence was unusual; they rarely left us for a weekend.

We jumped on our bikes, and I sat tall in my seat. An older boy had never asked me to go riding. This seemed out of the ordinary, but I was thrilled to be going by myself with him for a bike ride.

We rode down the street toward the outskirts of town. I lived "on the edge of nowhere" since right across the street was undeveloped land and there were only a few blocks of houses the other direction. A few blocks away was a farm and then the road turned one direction toward the highway north out of town. The other direction took you past a few more houses and then you were on a dirt road heading into the country. All this was familiar, safe territory for me.

Until this day.

He pulled over along the bushes by the farmer's field. I stopped my bike to see what he was doing. "Come sit over here by me," he said. I thought it was strange that he wanted to stop since we'd not ridden that far, but I complied.

What happened next changed my life forever. It damaged my view of love and relationships. It broke my relationship with him and many others I did not yet even know.

I remember him saying, "This is what people do who love each other. You love me, right?"

And then he pulled my pants down, unbuttoned his, and forcefully pulled me on top of him.

I also clearly remember him saying, "Don't tell anyone about this."

I was 9 years old.

How I was able to break his hold stymies me to this day. But I did. I pushed away from him, jumped on my bike, and rode home.

And I never told anyone about this. After all I was a "good girl" who did what she was told.

The first time I ever spoke of this was when Dave and I became engaged. However, even at that time, I brushed it off as "no big deal. I'd dealt with it. It was a one-time event. I wasn't really hurt."

I believed that lie. I chained it in a hidden corner of my prison, so far into the darkness that I believed it would never surface again. A nine-year-old child doesn't know how to deal with this type of pain. Because I never told anyone before Dave, for whatever the reason, I chose to shut down this part of myself.

But I didn't realize I was emotionally frozen at nine years old. The rancid sickness of that abuse now so commonplace in my system, I didn't sense the ongoing damage to my mind and soul.

The Bible says that freedom comes in the light¹. My prison walls, quickly constructed to hide the pain and confusion from this incident, inadvertently hid the light as well.

But the strength to maintain my "good" girl image was taking its toll. I just didn't realize how much.

As our conversation drew to a close, Mom quietly remarked, "I don't remember you ever going on a bike ride with him, honey. Are you sure?"

I was very sure. At least I thought I was.

"Why didn't you tell me? Did you think I wouldn't believe you?" I heard the pain in her voice and heart.

"I don't know, Mom. I usually told you everything. The only thing I can figure is that he told me not to tell anyone. So, being the obedient child I was, I didn't. I never told anyone until Dave and I were engaged. He's the first one I told. The details have never changed, so yes I believe this is a real memory. I can see where it happened."

But now I was second-guessing.

[I went over this conversation with the counselor later and was assured it was real, not imagined. I had too many specific details, too many vivid descriptions to have imagined this. A child wouldn't have those details. In fact, until a couple years ago, I believed my mom met at the door upon my return. But upon further reflection I remembered it was my grandmother who was at home which explained why Mom never knew about this bike ride. She wasn't there.]

My final call was to my sister. I needed her prayers and support. She was shocked, cried with me, and agreed to pray. She assured me I'd recover.

Exhaustion set in as the depression deepened. I'd never been so tired.

# When You Think
# You Want To Die

*For troubles surround me—too many to count! My sins pile up so high I can't see my way out. They outnumber the hairs on my head. I have lost all courage. Please, Lord, rescue me! Come quickly, Lord, and help me.*

*Psalm 40:12-13 NLT*

After the diagnosis, my descent into full-blown depression happened very quickly. As I curled up on the corner of the couch that night, feelings overwhelmed me in wave after wave. I felt like a small, abandoned child, very lost, very afraid.

No longer in my mid-forties, a wife, a mother, a soon-to-be grandmother, I was a child abandoned. The feeling of being lost and alone was like nothing I'd ever felt before. I know now this was PTSD, but I didn't know it then and I was very afraid. The monster under the bed felt real.

Emotionally, I was truly that child. I was going back and feeling the emotions but didn't know how to process them. I was beyond coping. I had nothing left to give Dave or anyone else. I was descending deeper into that hole, but I hadn't hit bottom yet.

Flashbacks came with increasing speed. The voices became intolerable, screaming venomous words at me, accusing me, bringing back memories of things I had done, failures in my life, mistakes that I had made. All of them accusing, beating me down, telling me that I was not worth anything, there was no point in living, that I was a burden to Dave, an anchor, an albatross. The word cacophony is not strong enough for how loud those voices were in my head.

There were times when I would be driving, yelling, screaming, and crying trying to overcome those condemning voices. I thought, *"I really am a lunatic."* I'm sure the people around me were wondering who this crazy woman was in the car next to them. I don't even know most of the time how I got from one place to another. I just know that I did. I'm sure there were guardian angels along the way that kept my car on the road and protected me.

In order to cope with this new level of pain, I turned off my emotions completely. My world turned gray. I couldn't hurt that much any more.

Instead, I crawled farther back into myself, shutting off the world around me, devoid of emotion, hiding deep in the shadows of my prison believing there I would be safe. There, I could escape the pain. There, no one would find me and hurt my anymore. There, I would be...alone.

I became a walking dead woman. My prison cell was on death row.

# When You Are Surprised By Kindness

*Yet you are near, O LORD, and all your commands are true.*

*Psalm 119:151*

I remember going back to my new job on the Monday following our intensive counseling.

Physically exhausted.
Emotionally destroyed.
Mentally reeling from the news.
Spiritually questioning everything I believed.

No longer did I feel qualified to do my job. No more confidence. I was totally broken, totally exposed. Like I had neon signs flashing "failure, liar, unworthy" over my head. The heavy weight of the diagnosis tightened the chains every day.

Little did I know my healing would begin at my new job, which I had only been at for a few days, and the team on which I'd been placed.

My immediate supervisor, a regional employee, just "happened" to be in the office for several meetings. In great fear and anticipating another rejection, I walked over to where she was preparing for another meeting, knocked on the door, and asked if I could have a few moments of her time. She invited me in, so I sat down and told her the results of my diagnosis. And waited for the condemnation followed by immediate termination I knew was coming.

*"After all, who would want an employee they barely knew who was this emotionally unstable?"* I told myself.

The condemnation never came. The Lord gave me a supervisor who knew what it was like to live with depression. She had a family member who had struggled with severe depression for many years. She was sympathetic, offered me hope, and offered the chance to end my contract if I felt I needed that. At the time I told her "No, I think I can do my work. However, I will need to take some time off every week for counseling sessions." She told me that was no problem but she would confer with our director.

When my phone rang the next morning, I recognized my director's number. Fearing sure rejection this time, I listened as she asked me several questions to which I responded honestly. What was the point to cover anything up, my stark reality left me totally exposed. I had no emotional reserves.

To my surprise, she was also familiar with depression and sympathetic to what I was going through. I'll never forget the graciousness of her words, "You take the time you need for the counseling. If, after a counseling session, it's just too much to come back to work, don't worry about it. We will figure it out. The important thing is you get the help you need and get healed." Hope started to slowly rise in my heart and mind.

Armed now with a grain of hope, I asked my coworkers if I could talk with them briefly. Still stumbling to find the words, I told them about my diagnosis and that I would be gone each week for counseling. Their immediate unconditional support, love, and concern brought on the tears once again. They were gracious, loving, and gentle with me. Even more than that, over the next months, they were careful to protect me. Never once did I hear a condemning word.

Within the next workday, I had my final conversation with the head of our department. Still not believing this graciousness would continue, I received the same care and concern as I received from every other person on my team. She affirmed my work and belief that I would recover and be an even stronger employee. When she prayed for me, that minuscule flicker of hope grew a bit stronger and brighter. It was a humbling experience.

God put me in a brand new job, with people I barely knew, who understood exactly where I was. A surprising sense of peace and safety engulfed me.

*"No matter how deep the pit into which I descend, I keep finding God there."*[1]

# When Nothing Makes Sense

*With all my heart I will praise you, O Lord my God.
I will give glory to your name forever, for your love
for me is very great. You have rescued me from the
depths of death.*

Psalm 86:12-13 NLT

Things needed to be done. Life needed to go on like:
washing dishes, paying bills, flipping through channels,
running errands, etc. In the midst of those tasks, so many
questions barraged me. They seemed to block my steps
right or left. They were there at every turn:

*"Now what?"*
*"What else do I need to deal with?"*
*"What damage have I done to my children because of
depression?"*
*"Have I done damage?"*
*"How long have I been depressed?"*
*"How long do I have to stay like this?"*
*"What will it be like to not be depressed?"*
*"How long will I have to take the medication?"*
*"Who is the 'not depressed' Kirsten?"*

*"How do I 'get over' depression?"*
*"Is this a family trait? Can I pass it on?"*

All questions that seemed to have no clear answers.

I've always been a good student, so I attempted to fight the depression the way I had worked through other problems, analytically. Simple really: Identify the issue, research possible solutions or outcomes, make the best choice based on the information at hand, and move forward. But as much as I tried to find a way around the depression, nothing worked. Depression wasn't something I could fix on my own. I prayed for healing. I begged for it.

Depression is an ugly disease. Add to that the stigmas attached to it, the misunderstandings surrounding the disease, and the merciless trap closes on its victims.

Nowadays, we tend to throw the word "depression", or "depressed", around any time we are sad, bummed out, or have "the blues." But depression is much more insidious than "the blues."

According to helpguide.org[1]:

> *"Depression is a common and debilitating mood disorder*
> *that is affecting more and more people around the world...*
> *people of all ages experience symptoms of depression...*
> *Depression varies from person to person, but there are*
> *some common signs and symptoms. It's important to*
> *remember that these symptoms can be part of life's normal*
> *lows. But the more symptoms you have, the stronger they*

*are, and the longer they've lasted—the more likely it is that you're dealing with depression. When these symptoms are overwhelming and disabling, that's when it's time to seek help."*

While this disease affects millions of people, it is still greatly misunderstood by the general populace.

## Signs or Symptoms of Depression:[2]

- **Feelings of helplessness and hopelessness.** A bleak outlook—nothing will ever get better and there's nothing you can do to improve your situation.
- **Loss of interest in daily activities.** No interest in former hobbies, pastimes, social activities, or sex. You've lost your ability to feel joy and pleasure.
- **Appetite or weight changes.** Significant weight loss or weight gain—a change of more than 5% of body weight in a month.
- **Sleep changes.** Either insomnia, especially waking in the early hours of the morning, or oversleeping.
- **Anger or irritability.** Feeling agitated, restless, or even violent. Your tolerance level is low, your temper short, and everything and everyone gets on your nerves.
- **Loss of energy.** Feeling fatigued, sluggish, and physically drained. Your whole body may feel heavy, and even small tasks are exhausting or take longer to complete.
- **Self-loathing.** Strong feelings of worthlessness or guilt. You harshly criticize yourself for perceived faults and mistakes.
- **Reckless behavior.** You engage in escapist behavior such as substance abuse, compulsive gambling, reckless driving, or dangerous sports.
- **Concentration problems.** Trouble focusing, making decisions, or remembering things.
- **Unexplained aches and pains.** An increase in physical complaints such as headaches, back pain, aching muscles, and stomach pain.

There is a feeling of emptiness that makes it difficult to function on a daily basis. In my case, the accompanying fatigue increased my inability to function normally. And this fatigue was more than simply being tired. It was a bone-weariness, a sense of impending doom, a total inability to concentrate on anything for any period of time. In many ways I felt like my mind had been hijacked. I've since learned that this sense is a common symptom of depression.

For me, depression was an endless black hole, bereft of any sound.

Mistakenly I thought that the medication would make a big difference. It didn't. At least not as quickly as I wanted.

While there was probably a chemical component to my depression, the root causes could not be remedied by medication. That healing would require absolute honesty on my part, professional counseling, and the consistent support of our Team and family.

My descent continued. I was more frightened than I'd ever been but I had no way to stop the descent. No way to grab onto anything or anyone to break my fall. I knew the bottom was coming but I didn't know if I would survive the crash.

Gone were my quick, spiritual clichés I'd been so free to spout to others.

Gone was my flimsy assurance that all would be fine. God wouldn't bring anything to me that I couldn't handle. Right? This time, it felt like He did.

Gone was my tepid belief system. And because of this, I felt extreme fear and isolation.

I couldn't pray.
I couldn't read my Bible.
Nothing made sense anymore.

I had believed that a "true" believer in Christ wouldn't suffer with suicidal depression. If "all things work together for good to those who love the Lord"[3] then how could you be depressed to the point that you would want to take your own life? It didn't make sense to me, so I determined it wasn't possible.

Yet, here I was suicidally depressed. How could that be?

The voices began their barrage:

*"And you call yourself a Christian?"*
*"Failure! Can't even be a good Christian."*
*"Guess God isn't real like you thought."*
*"A good God wouldn't let this happen to you."*
*"Worthless."*

The battle was just beginning; I was quickly losing ground. This enemy was a monster I'd never faced before. And that frightened me as I slid further into the darkness of my prison.

# When You Have
# To Wake Up

*But deal well with me, O Sovereign Lord, for the sake of your own reputation! Rescue me because you are so faithful and good. For I am poor and needy, and my heart is full of pain.*

Psalm 109:21-22 NLT

My personal counseling began two weeks after we finished our intensive marriage sessions. Rob was insistent that I begin treatment ASAP.

I remember meeting my new counselor and robotically answering her questions. I remember not wanting to be there. I remember defending my husband but not myself. I remember feeling dead inside.

She asked several questions which I answered mostly with "fine." If you've ever seen the movie, *The Italian Job*, they define "fine" as "Freaked out, Insecure, Neurotic, and Emotional." An apt description for me at the time. My counselor told me I needed to learn to identify my emotions and I wasn't allowed to use the word "fine" again. Now I was flummoxed.

I didn't know how I felt. In reality I didn't feel anything. But now I had an assignment. Each day I had to write in my journal the answers to five questions:

1. Today I feel:
2. When I feel this way, the thoughts that go through my head are:
3. When I feel this way and think these thoughts, I want to:
4. My choice today is to:
5. My prayer today is:

I'd never been very good at journaling consistently so this was not something I wanted to do. Most of my journaling attempts in the past had been historical, more factual in nature. "Today we spent time at the pool with Joe and Sara. It was a terribly hot day so the pool was a wonderful relief...." Nothing about how I felt or even remotely personal. Just a record that someone could read years from now and get a "glimpse into the life." How could I journal my feelings when I didn't know how I felt?

> "Dead people feel nothing."
> Kary Oberbrunner

Plus, I didn't want to know how I felt.

My weekly counseling sessions were emotionally grueling. We started by reviewing the events that led up to our intensive counseling. I was so tired of recounting that story! Each time I did, the scab ripped off the painful gash in my heart.

But it wasn't enough to go over Dave's addiction and my depression diagnosis, with Godly wisdom, she went back through the events leading up to this crisis. And as we walked through the events of the previous year and beyond, I discovered how many major life events had stacked on top of each other. Some of them were thrilling; others were heart-wrenching.

Memories started flooding back....

Our daughter was engaged! It was such an exciting time for all of us. We talked about how we would use technology to allow my dad to "attend" her wedding. We knew he wouldn't be able to travel to the wedding because of a heart condition, but surely there was some way for him to "be there" while remaining in the comfort of his own home. Dave and Eric started brainstorming options.

Just a week or so later my office phone rang. Picking up the phone, I heard my sister tell me that Dad was back in the hospital. Something in her voice told me this wasn't good.

We'd just been there a few weeks ago to see Dad and Mom. While we were there I recorded some video of my

Dad telling stories of growing up in northern Minnesota as a first generation American, his time in the navy during World War II, his marriage to Mom, and his salvation experience. I knew this footage would prove to be priceless to our family legacy.

Hearing my sister that day, there was a strong prompting in my spirit to get there as fast as possible. Things weren't good for Dad. I hung up the phone and called Dave who agreed to call the travel agent to see what flights were available that day. While Dave did that, I went to my boss and explained the situation. I needed to go as soon as I could get a flight.

Our receptionist poked her head in my boss' office to let me know Dave was on the phone. Excusing myself, I headed to my office, picked up the phone, and learned there was a flight at 5:00 p.m. If I left the office right now, ran home and packed a bag, I'd just make the flight.

I did make the flight and arrived at my sister's home that evening. There wasn't time to let them know I was coming until I landed at the airport in their hometown.

My sister was surprised when I called to say I was in town and asked me why I had come so quickly. I told her, "I felt the Spirit telling me to go right away, so I came."

Dad had a couple of bad days but eventually began to improve. He couldn't come home from the hospital, however, until he could do some things on his own.

He was so weak. Mom tasked my sister and me with research-
ing some skilled care facilities. We had limited time to do
so before the hospital wanted to release him. After touring
several, we made our best recommendation to Mom and
she agreed. Papers were signed to move Dad to a facility,
thankfully, near my mom and sister.

I'll never forget the day the medical team moved Dad to
the facility. It was horrible. I hated it, but I knew we couldn't
bring him home.

The room we'd seen and agreed would be good for Dad was
large and airy feeling. It could accommodate two patients,
but we were led to believe Dad would be by himself. There
was a comfortable couch that Mom could use while visiting
Dad as well as a couple other comfy chairs. It was in the
new wing and felt quite home-like. We'd assured Mom of
the comfort and quality of the room. However, the room
Dad was assigned was not at all like the room we'd been
led to believe he'd be assigned. It was not in the new wing.
It was much smaller and cramped. We were so disappointed,
but couldn't get them to budge on his accommodations.

We spent a majority of each day there with Dad. Some days
were good and encouraging, but most were not. I could see
that Dad was very weak.

One day, I took Dad to the courtyard where he could be
outside for a while and enjoy some nature. Pushing Dad in
his wheelchair, we explored one of the hallways to another
wing, when Dad noticed some men working on the founda-
tion for a new part of the building. I'll never forget his words,

"They're the lucky ones. Out there working hard." The longing in his voice was palpable. Work was fun to Dad. Sitting in this wheelchair, not able to do much for himself, was not.

Dad and I talked more while enjoying the sunshine and then I took him back to his room. Mom arrived shortly after that, so I left them to visit together.

The last time I saw Dad, I helped him get from his wheelchair into his bed. He'd developed some sores so we needed to change his position. In the process of working on that together, we both got to laughing so hard we couldn't do anything. That was the last time I felt my dad's arms around me and heard him tell me how much he loved me.

I told Dad, "The next time I see you will be at home."

When I flew home the next day, I left believing I'd never see my dad alive on this earth again. The truth was I'd see him at home—in heaven. I began praying that God would take him home and end his suffering. How do you pray for someone to die? But, I did. The suffering was too much to watch, and Dad was so weak.

# When Death Smacks You In The Face

*Precious in the sight of the Lord is the death of his faithful servants.*

Psalm 116:15

For months we'd been planning a trip to Europe for our 25th wedding anniversary. Nate's university adventure gave us a great excuse to see a part of the world I'd dreamed about for almost my entire life.

Dad and I had talked about our plans for this trip. He encouraged me to go and enjoy it. When I asked him what I could bring back for him, he said, "Just lots of pictures and your memories."

Three weeks later, Dad entered eternity. A little under three months before our daughter's wedding. And three weeks before Nate planned to head to Austria.

Dad had spent that day in the hospital having returned there a week earlier due to complications the occurred while in the care facility. Both my brothers had been to see him, my eldest brother left the day before. My mom, sister, and brother-in-law had spent a good portion of that day with Dad filled with lots of laughter and joking around. Dad was in good spirits, and kissed my mom goodbye when she left.

Late that evening, Dad slipped away in his sleep. He went to sleep on earth and woke up fully alive in heaven.

My sister called just after midnight to let me know Dad had died. Two thoughts screamed at once: "My dad is gone", utter sadness, and "Thank you, Jesus," relief! He wouldn't have to suffer any more.

I don't know how you can have these diametric thoughts at the same time, but I did. I hurt so badly, but I was so thankful he wasn't suffering.

D.L. Moody said, "Someday you will read in the papers, 'D. L. Moody of East Northfield is dead.' Don't you believe a word of it! At that moment I shall be more alive than I am now...."[1] I now understood the truth of this statement. My dad was fully alive and strong once again. Out there working hard. I have no doubt that I will see him again.

But my pain at the separation I felt on this earth was undeniable. My dad was gone. I'd never hear his voice again. Never hear his contagious, spontaneous laugh. Never feel his arms holding me so preciously. I ached. I already missed him.

We made some calls the next morning to some friends in our town who had been praying for Dad's healing. Several of them came by the house just to sit with us and let me cry.

The Jewish people have a custom of "sitting shiva[2]," a time of honoring the death by simply being with the family and providing food for the grieving family. These friends, though not Jewish and maybe not even aware of this custom, did exactly that. They joined us in our grief and provided for our physical needs.

I fully believed in the hope of the resurrection. Yet, as I would learn later, I didn't fully grieve. Instead, I was lost, moving deeper into the darkness.

# When Too Much
# Happens At Once

*My soul is weary with sorrow.*
*Psalm 119:28*

The three weeks prior to leaving for Europe were spent in Minnesota for Dad's first memorial service, then back home for wedding planning and shopping with Erin, and finally off to Phoenix, Arizona, for Dad's second memorial service. I arrived home April 16, worked April 17, then left in the wee hours of April 18 with Dave and Nate for Austria.

I've never been so utterly fatigued in my life. So fatigued that I went to the doctor between the two memorial services to get help with my insomnia. I wasn't sleeping more than two hours a night. How can a person be so desperately exhausted and not able to sleep?

As we boarded our flight to "cross the pond", I was thankful for the sleeping pills the doctor prescribed. I needed to sleep and sleep well. And I did. Another perk of my long, deep sleep was a speedy adjustment to the time change.

We arrived in Frankfurt very early in the morning. We had a several hour layover, which gave us time to explore the airport, sleep a little more, eat, and then board our final flight to Salzburg, Austria, where we would stay for a couple of days before heading to Schladming on the train.

Erin and Casey's wedding date was a mere three weeks after we got back from Europe. We left home with the agreement we would check our email once a day when we could find an internet cafe. Any wedding-related questions would have to be handled via email. If necessary, we could call home if an email wouldn't suffice.

While Dave and I looked forward to the "empty nest," we had married young and had children right away, we also wondered aloud about what our life would be like. This was it. Our last child to leave home.

"What will we do with our time?"
"How will we adjust to the silence?"
"What will it be like to keep track of only our schedules?"

We anticipated our lives losing some vitality while we slowed our pace. Boy, were we wrong.

Our B&B accommodations in Salzburg, Haus am Moos[1], were lovely—basically an entire apartment for the three of us. Breathtaking views surrounded us. We were in Salzburg! A dream of mine coming true.

We dropped Nate off at Tauernhof and headed back to Salzburg to start the rest of our vacation. This was our 25th anniversary after all!

We were thrilled to be in Europe. Yet, there was a cloud over this trip: grief over my dad's death and grief over leaving my youngest child alone in a foreign country. Nate was thrilled. I was thrilled for him, but my heart hurt.

*"Would we really board a plane and head back home and leave him here across the ocean?"*

I knew the answer to that question because I'd done it two years earlier when Eric went to school in New Zealand. And I knew boarding that plane would take all the strength I could muster. My mother's heart hurt thinking about leaving my child behind, in a foreign country, for the next ten months.

We arrived home three weeks to the day before Erin and Casey's wedding. No time to pause or rest, we had to quickly help with the final wedding preparations.

The next three weeks were spent focused on our only daughter's wedding. Erin had planned everything so well. Yet, with the normal bridal showers, fittings, and last minute things to be done, there was no time to grieve, let alone think.

So many emotional milestones happening within a compressed time frame. So many memories to capture. My emotions were fragile and crumbling. I knew I had to make it through the wedding festivities before I could give way to the jumble of emotions I was holding inside.

# When You Aren't Prepared

*When life is heavy and hard to take, go off by yourself.*
*Enter the silence. Bow in prayer. Don't ask questions:*
*Wait for hope to appear.*

Lamentations 3:28-29 THE MESSAGE

Our daughter's wedding day was finally here! My heart felt as full as the nearby hotel, filled to the brim with family and friends from far and wide, eager to share this special time with us.

The church was decorated. Erin's gorgeous gown was hanging in the closet. Tux fittings were complete. I'd even found a dress to wear.

This wedding was the first major family event since my dad's death. Welcome, joyful emotions flooded over me as not-so-welcome ones made themselves known too. I thought back to the joy and the pain of Erin's birth not so long ago. Isn't it odd how major life events often stimulate such mixed emotions?

My baby's birth was quickly approaching.

I was very uncomfortable and getting rather impatient to deliver this baby. At my appointment, the doctor noticed the swelling in my hands and feet. After finishing the exam, he asked the nurse to check my blood pressure again as it was a little high when I first arrived.

Reviewing that reading, he turned to me and said, "I don't like what I'm seeing. You are showing signs of toxemia. I want you to go home, get your bag, and go straight to the hospital. We are going to induce you. The good news is you're going to have your baby."

I burst into tears. Toxemia. I was scared. I didn't want to lose my baby. Dave drove us to our apartment to get my hospital bag which was packed and ready to go. With my pregnancy hormones in overdrive, fear hijacked my mind.

They started the induction and the labor pains went from tolerable to intolerable in the span of minutes. By about 10:00 p.m. the doctor decided to slow it down and try again in the morning as nothing much was happening. He sent Dave home to sleep and told me to rest as well because tomorrow would be a long day. I didn't get much sleep.

Our daughter's birth was hard, but she arrived safely. I was so thankful. We now had a beautiful baby girl with lots of dark hair, so awake and observant. She stole my heart and wrapped her daddy's heart around her little finger in the space of a breath.

In the hours after her birth, several friends came to see her and us. While the final visitor was there, I started having some pretty strong cramps. After they left, I rang for the nurse to get some pain meds to deal with the rapidly increasing pain. When the nurse came in to perform a routine check on me, I passed a large clot and started bleeding profusely.

I remember hearing "Code Blue." "I can't get a blood pressure."

I remember giving Dave the number to the church so he could call them to pray—it was Wednesday night prayer meeting time.

I saw three doctors, all prepped for surgery, rush into my room that was now packed with quickly moving people. Someone asked Dave to leave the room. But then an older nurse asked, "Where's her husband?" (I was desperately looking for Dave.) "He's the most important person in this room right now. Where is he?" She quickly brought Dave back into the room. I found his eyes and stared at him thinking, *"If I close my eyes I won't wake up..."* Hearing "we need blood now." Feeling cold.

I woke up in a birthing surgical recovery room with wires, cuffs, and equipment attached everywhere I could see. And I hurt. Turns out, I was bleeding out.

I'm told my hospital room looked like a war zone. Evidently when I passed that blood clot, it was severe, sudden, and very dramatic. Dave said one of the doctors literally ran to the basement blood bank to get three pints of blood for me. That's why I felt cold. They were hand pumping the blood into me as fast as possible because I didn't have a blood pressure.

Our pastor arrived at my original room and thought he was too late. He told me later that he thought I was dead. Someone spotted him outside my room and told him where he could find me. I remember seeing him in the surgical recovery room, but only vaguely.

Dave told me that as this whole scene unfolded all he could think was he was losing his wife and would have to raise his new beautiful baby girl on his own. And he had no clue how to do that.

However, I was miraculously alive.

I took in a deep breath. Thankful to be alive on this, my daughter's wedding day.

My siblings were all here with my mom. But my heart mourned the loss of my dad and the absence of our son in Europe. Our family was missing a couple of beloved people.

Erin planned a special tribute for my dad. When she told me about it, I was so touched. It was perfect. Simple, quiet, but her own tribute for her beloved grandpa.

The wedding day was lovely. So many fun activities. Our house was full of special friends. What a blessing to have them all together again in our home. My heart soared with joy. I told myself to fully enter into this day, the day my only daughter was getting married. I wanted to soak it all in, not miss a moment.

But I wasn't prepared for the emotions of this day. Not just the emotions of my oldest child and only daughter getting married, but the added emotions of my dad's death.

I wasn't prepared.

Erin was absolutely gorgeous and radiant. When Dave prayed over her at the church prior to the wedding my heart burst with joy for her and for all God had done in her life to bring her to this day. Erin was radiantly beautiful in Him.

I went to the hallway to get ready to head down the aisle ahead of Dave and Erin. Nate, in Austria (it was the middle of the night), was all set to watch his sister walk down the aisle through the technological marvel of Skype. Once seated I would pick up the laptop and turn it so he could see Erin walk down the aisle.

It was then I looked over and saw Mom sitting with the other grandparents. The only widow in the group of four sets of grandparents. And the tears began. How I missed my dad! How I longed to see him. He would have been so excited for this day for his Erin. Joy and pain. My mother smiled at me. She was holding herself together fairly well though I could see the grief in her eyes.

At last it was time. I rushed back to my place in line and we headed down the aisle. Reaching my place at the front of the chapel, I waved to Nate on the laptop screen. Then I slid in beside the laptop and whispered to him that I would turn the screen so he could see Erin.

Suddenly, the music commanded our attention, signaling the bride was soon to appear. My stomach flipped. Every molecule in the room seemed charged with joy. I stood, turned with the laptop, to behold my husband escorting our beautiful daughter down the aisle. Erin looked over and saw Nate on the screen and blew him a kiss. She was stunning.

The ceremony and reception were a wonderful celebration. I tried to take it all in, to capture the moments as one takes snapshots, but there was simply too much. It was beautiful; a carnival of laughter, love, bright colors, joy, fun, and then, almost without notice, it was done.

The next morning, my family came for brunch before they left town. It was so good to laugh, reminisce, and soak up those few hours with them in our home. I was so grateful.

After everyone left, I went to rest for a bit. That's when the tears came, when the emotions of the last couple of months poured out from my eyes—an unstoppable flood. Thankfully, Dave sensed it coming so he wasn't surprised.

And, even more importantly, he knew how to give me space to let it out.

I needed time now to myself to restore. There was nothing left to give to anyone. I needed time to heal.

The problem was I didn't know how to grieve, how to heal, how to deal honestly with the emotions, pain, and life changes of the past few months. My world was about to explode into fractured shards.

The prison mouth opened wider eager to suck me deeper into its slimy depths.

And I wasn't prepared. I was completely clueless.

# When The Past Heals The Present

*In my distress I called to the Lord; I cried to my God for help. From his temple he heard my voice; my cry came before him, into his ears.*

Psalm 18:6

O ne of the first major tests of our restoration process came within a few months of our intensive counseling.

Dave and I were doing much better with our communication. We were getting bolder at speaking truthfully from our hearts. We were praying together every morning before we started our day. We were guarding our time so we could process together what we were learning with our Restoration Team and through my continued counseling.

The depression still had me in a hammer-lock which meant it was imperative that I not withdraw even more. I was learning to honestly express how I was emotionally, mentally, and physically feeling each day. Dave was sensitive to the physical struggle, often performing extra household chores to alleviate some physical stress. Keeping the house neat helped settle my mental state.

However, despite the progress we were making individually and together, we were about to face a challenge to our progress.

One winter evening early in the new year, we received a text that said, "She said yes!" We were so excited! Our son, Eric, had just proposed to his girlfriend. Dave and I waited for his promised phone call to hear how it all came together.

We all knew the proposal was coming. He'd flown across the country to surprise her, taking the weekend off from work and school.

He'd made reservations at a favorite restaurant near her home. He'd ordered a beautiful bouquet of flowers to be placed on their table. The maître d' had a bottle of champagne chilling, ready to rush to the table at the appropriate moment.

His girlfriend thought he was simply coming to visit, and since he'd be hungry when he got there, they would go out for dinner.

Everything was going as planned, until he dropped the ring box from his pocket as he was getting out of the car! Quickly he snatched it a moment before she turned and saw it. So close!

When they got to the table, Eric's girlfriend noticed the beautiful flowers but didn't think it too out of the ordinary until Eric dropped to one knee and proposed. She let out an excited squeal and said, "Yes!"

At the end of the weekend, Eric flew back to his college campus, feeling on top of the world.

After he arrived back at campus, he called. I couldn't wait to talk with him and hear all about the proposal and her response.

"Mom," I heard the rasp and wheezing through the phone connection, "I'm having problems breathing."

"It started getting bad on the flight back. I've taken my inhaler but it's not helping. What do I do? It's really hard to breathe."

I felt my heart begin to pound. Adrenaline surged through my body. My baby was in trouble. He couldn't breathe!

I asked a few more questions, found out the campus clinic was closed, but his roommate was there and had a car available.

"Go to the nearest Emergency Room. You need help now," I said. "Have your roommate call me when you get there and keep me posted. Go right now!"

As we hung up the phone, I began to tremble violently. Immediately I grabbed the laptop computer to search for available flights. I had to get to him. There were no flights available that night; the earliest was the next morning. Frustration and panic mounted.

A flashback cascaded over me.

Eric was 4 weeks old. My parents had left a few days earlier, and we were adjusting to our new home and being parents of two beautiful children. Mom had called to see how things were going, so we were happily chatting on the phone.

Suddenly, Erin, our two-year-old, came running to me crying, "The baby can't breathe!"

I dropped the phone and ran to Eric's bedroom to find him choking, not getting enough air. I ran back to the phone, grabbed it, told my mom what was happening, and asked her what to do. I was panicking and couldn't think.

"Turn him over and whack him on the back between his shoulder blades," she said. I did but he was still gasping for air.

"He's still not breathing right," I cried into the phone.

"You need to get help. Call for help," Mom said and we hung up the phone.

I called the doctor and heard, "He needs to get to the hospital. Can you get him to the hospital?"

Dave was at work and had our only car. "Wait," I thought, "I can call our neighbor, looks like they are home."

I called our neighbor. She came right over, along with her husband, who agreed to watch Erin.

I called Dave's office where one of his interns answered. Dave was away from his desk so I quickly told the intern that the baby was in trouble and I was taking him to the hospital. This was an emergency. Dave needed to meet me there.

My neighbor and I jumped in her car and headed to the hospital. Just four blocks from our home, Eric stopped breathing and started turning blue. My neighbor sped up and turned toward the fire station, horn blaring. We needed immediate help! My baby wasn't breathing.

Don't ask me why I didn't call an ambulance to begin with since the hospital was in the next town. I don't know. I only heard "You need to get the baby to the hospital," so I did. Looking back, I remember my neighbor asking if we shouldn't call an ambulance. At least one person was thinking, though I didn't listen.

As we pulled up to the fire station, I remembered this was a volunteer fire department, not normally staffed. Yet, God in His mercy had a police officer there getting a cup of coffee. He came to the entrance when he heard us honking. I ran up to him and said, "Please help me! My baby isn't breathing!"

The police officer grabbed Eric, ran inside, flipped him over and began to work with him, while calling dispatch for help. In less than a minute, an EMT arrived and took over.

My neighbor held me close as my knees buckled. Tears streaming down my face, I watched my helpless child and the two men working to save his life.

Finally, they looked over at me and said he was breathing normally, now on oxygen. They loaded Eric and me in the ambulance and headed for the hospital in the next town. My neighbor followed in her car.

When we arrived at the ER, Dave was already there. The EMT rushed Eric into the ER and gave the physician the update. Evidently, he'd suctioned Eric's lungs and that's when he started breathing again.

Through a series of events, one of which entailed calling our family doctor directly because the ER physician didn't believe Eric had really stopped breathing, we ended up at Children's Hospital. Eric had several problems: apnea—cessation of breathing, especially during sleep; bradycardia—an abnormally slow heartbeat; and reflux—where stomach contents leak back into the esophagus. I was told we could have easily lost him to SIDS—Sudden Infant Death Syndrome.

Several miracles occurred this day.

Erin, a two-year-old, understood her baby brother was in trouble and came immediately to me for help.

The police officer was at the unmanned station.

Unbeknownst to me, the dispatcher he called that day was his wife. He brilliantly called her directly instead of going through central dispatch, which saved several minutes.

The EMT on call lived across the street from the fire station.

Our doctor knew me well enough to know I wouldn't make something like this up. He knew Eric needed immediate attention and ordered him transported to Children's Hospital.

The medical team at Children's took immediate action to discover the root cause of this episode even though Eric looked totally healthy when we arrived.

A week later, we left Children's Hospital with Eric, on a heart monitor, understanding how close we came to losing him.

God spared our son's life.

When my grown-up Eric called that day, once again struggling to breathe, Dave was working in the shop. I called to him to come in right away.

Between that call and his arrival, I lost all emotional control. Frustrated tears mingled with panic. I began to sob and yell at God.

*"No! You can't take him! I can't bear it. Why can't I be there to take care of him? This is my baby! No, you can't take him! You can't! You just can't! Please God, save my son. I can't bear another loss."*

Through heaving sobs, I tried to tell Dave what was happening. It was so disjointed and jumbled Dave couldn't understand and thought Eric had died. Finally, I was able to calm down enough to be coherent.

No, Eric wasn't dead but he was having trouble breathing. He was in trouble. I needed to get to him. Now!

And Dave began to pray for God's intervention, peace, and wisdom.

We looked at flights for the next day in case we needed to go. And we waited for a call.

Rather quickly, we received a call from Eric's roommate. Eric was being seen. He'd update us more when he knew more.

Turns out Eric had pleurisy aggravated by the plane trip. He'd thought it was just a cold. He was going to be fine. God answered my frantic prayer and understood my mother's heart.

For the first time, I hadn't stuffed my fear and emotions. I'd fully experienced them. This realization encouraged me that I was making emotional progress. I hadn't pushed my pain down or tried to spiritualize it to lessen the impact. I was freaked out. So I freaked out.

> I hadn't pushed my pain down or tried to spiritualize it to lessen the impact. I was freaked out. So I freaked out.

At my counseling session the next day, my counselor affirmed the evidence of healing:

- Was my reaction dramatic? Yes
- Overly so? Maybe
- Healthy? Yes
- Sign of progress? Definitely!
- Sinful? No!

I still had a long road of recovery in this depression journey, but I was on the road.

Sometimes you have to celebrate the wins even when they seem insignificant or present themselves in an unusual way.

I learned God was able to handle my fear and my tantrum. He didn't strike me dead. He didn't belittle me. He gave me peace. He understood my fragile mother's heart and held me close. And He held my child even closer.

Several miracles saved Eric that day when he was four-weeks-old, and now another miracle occurred all these years later.

The tears flow more freely these days. Sometimes they feel disproportionate to the situation. But they are flowing, no longer pent up and festering inside my mind and heart.

I was waking up, becoming alive. I wouldn't choose the pain except it proved that I was finally present.

I'd spent too many years holding the pain inside. Too many years trying to prove my faith in God by being strong and stoic. Too many years believing the lie that keeping up appearances is more spiritual than authenticity, that true faith doesn't question the bad things that happen.

Finally, I let myself feel. I let myself breathe.

# When Jesus Redeems Your Past

*You, Lord, are my lamp; the Lord turns my dark-
ness into light.*

*2 Samuel 22:29*

Through my journaling and counseling I realized I never learned to grieve. Due to my early abuse, I'd shut down that portion of my emotions in order to deal with my pain. Though not necessarily intentional, it had devastating consequences.

The dictionary defines grief as *"keen mental suffering or distress over affliction or loss; sharp sorrow; painful regret; a cause or occasion of keep distress or sorrow."* My abuse could be characterized as a cause of deep distress. Since a nine-year-old has no idea how to process this, I simply shut down that part of my emotions. Essentially, I made a vow to myself (without realizing it) that I'd never be hurt this way again.

But I couldn't keep that vow.

My counselor took me back to the day of my abuse—I remembered the details and began to tremble violently—as she asked, "Where is Jesus?" Not "where was Jesus" because this was still very much present day. The memory so vivid my senses were fully alive. My counselor knew it was critical for me to see Jesus present, to redeem this memory, in order to heal the deep wound.

Pushing through the fear, shame, and pain I forced myself to look for Jesus. I could hardly breathe. I felt my heart rapidly pounding. My hands became clammy.

Suddenly, with HDTV-like clarity, I saw Him standing just beyond the left shoulder of my abuser. He was weeping. Weeping.

Jesus was weeping for my pain. He was weeping for the pain within my abuser.

Jesus understood the devastation of this abuse.

While the pain from my abuse was still there, I no longer felt alone. I no longer felt ashamed. Jesus saw what happened. His tears washed away the sin I felt. It wasn't my fault. I hadn't done anything to deserve the abuse. And the abuse was real. But it was not mine to carry alone. He was there.

I saw myself push away from my abuser and run. That's when I realized Jesus protected me from further harm. My abuser physically towered over me, yet he never pursued me when I ran.

Knowing Jesus was there, redeemed my memory. I realized that Jesus was weeping for the cruel bond of sin that chained me to shame and guilt. Not only me, but also my abuser. He came to set me, and all of humanity, free from sin's control. In that moment of abuse, the enemy of my soul believed he'd won the battle. Yet, Jesus died to redeem that moment, that sin, that pain. Jesus redeemed it.

Another chain broken. Another breath of freedom.

As I continued to journal, and work through materials provided by my counselor, another deeply buried memory surfaced with sudden clarity.

It was my first year at college. I was young, naive, and living in a big city for the first time.

I attended a Christian college where I participated in several extracurricular activities. One of these was visiting a nursing home in the area once a week with a team that provided a "Sunday service" to the residents. My role was to play the piano so the residents could sing some of their favorite hymns, *Amazing Grace, Great is Thy Faithfulness, Fairest Lord Jesus*, and *Near the Cross*. While many would sing, some would simply sit with eyes closed and smile, tears wetting their weathered cheeks. It was such a sweet sound coupled with a beautiful display of silent worship.

They seemed so starved for someone to care, for a moment of joy. They would light up when we'd walk in the main gathering space. My heart broke each week. The hardworking staff seemed caring, but there was so much for them to do. I remember one resident in particular who would follow me with her eyes. She was so starved for human touch. I seem to remember discovering that no one came to visit her. The team and I would walk around and hold hands or give hugs. Basically we learned to just be in their presence for those few hours each week.

On one of these visits, I left the main area to use the restroom. On my way back to talk with several of the ladies I'd gotten to know, an orderly stopped me. He was a young man, a good-looking guy, and he started talking to me, seeming to want to know more about me. But in a matter of minutes, he crossed the normal "personal space" boundary between us to the point that I was backed up against a wall. My heart began to pound as I sensed danger. I desperately looked for someone nearby to catch their attention. But the hall was strangely empty.

Before I had a chance to make my move, he made his. I thrust his hand off my breast, pushed as hard as I could against him, and quickly headed toward the common room, repeating over and over to myself "You're okay, you're okay, you're okay."

But I wasn't okay.

Dan Allender, in *The Wounded Heart*, says, "Sexual abuse is damaging no matter how the victim's body is violated."[1]

By the time I got back to my dorm room, I managed to scrape together the courage to tell a couple girls on my floor who then took me to see the dean. I was so embarrassed. *"What had I done to bring this on myself?"* I was so ashamed. Telling her what happened was torture. She believed me but had to ask some probing questions. Questions that made me feel like I'd had a role to play in his inappropriate behavior. I felt my soul climbing into its protective chamber and crawling deeper into the darkness.

I didn't return to that particular nursing home again. But I lived in fear that he would show up on campus because he knew where I went to college.

Living life looking over your shoulder is exhausting.

# When You Learn To Grieve

*Be merciful to me, Lord, for I am in distress; my eyes grow weak with sorrow, my soul and body with grief.*

*Psalm 31:9*

Later when reading *The Wounded Heart*, I read about my emotional state and the hidden internal vow I'd made.

*"Hiding the past always involves denial, denial of the past is always a denial of God. To forget your personal history is tantamount to trying to forget yourself and the journey that God has called you to live."[1]*

This type of reaction is very common for victims of abuse. The first few weeks of counseling dealt with grieving those memories and experiences that I'd buried all these years. Journaling about this and discussing these memories with my counselor helped me learn many things.

- I learned that crying doesn't equal grieving.
- I learned that grief results when life takes a sudden unexpected directional shift from which you can never return to the original path.

- I learned that the grief process is very individualized—no one experiences grief the same way.
- I learned that grief never really ceases; you simply learn to keep going. You don't "get over" grief.
- I learned that grief is normal and not to be feared.

But understanding is one thing. Applying these principles is much different. Because I'd shut off this portion of my mind and emotions when I was nine years old, the memories surfacing now had to be grieved. Over the next several weeks, each buried traumatic event that surfaced had to be examined and grieved as if it had just happened.

Growing up is hard enough the first time. But allowing my emotional state to grow up to my current physical age during the next several weeks took quite the toll. When one part of your being is not functioning at optimal capacity, the other parts of your being begin to suffer as well.

Physically and emotionally all I wanted to do was sleep now. As more memories surfaced that needed to be grieved, my depression deepened.

Growing up was wonderful. We lived in a small town where you knew almost everyone. Neighbors looked after neighbors. Kids were watched by all the adults around them. You couldn't get away with anything because someone was always around to keep you in line.

Safe. Secure. Loved.

No doubt about that.

One special treat was living six blocks from my paternal grandparents. I could easily walk there or ride my bike. I didn't know then how unique and special this was because at the time most of my friends' grandparents lived in the same town as well. It was normal for us and we called everyone "Grandma" or "Grandpa"—it didn't matter if they weren't really yours.

My grandparents were always around. Imagine my shock when my grandpa died. That was my first experience with death. And it hurt. Unquestionably hurt.

I loved being cradled safely in Grandpa's arms, snugged up tight next to his chest. I loved the feel of his work-worn hands, the gentle timbre of his voice. I looked for his special smile just for me. Grandpa was a constant part of my life.

Going to Grandpa and Grandma's house after he died, I walked in expecting to be greeted with a hug, a kiss, and a smile from Grandma. Like normal. But she didn't. Instead, she was weeping uncontrollably. There were lots of people there and not just family. I felt afraid and bewildered. I don't even remember her acknowledging my presence. I just remember her continual sobs.

As a young child, I didn't know how to process this. I didn't go to the funeral. Much later, I would visit my grandpa's burial site. But I didn't understand. One minute Grandpa was alive and laughing and then suddenly he was no longer there.

It hurt too much, so I wrapped up my pain and bewilderment and hid them deep down inside.

Just a few short years later I faced another death. My maternal grandmother died. She'd been sick, but her death was unexpected. Since my mom's parents lived about an hour away, Dad and Mom traveled to my grandparents. I was left home with my siblings. I missed Dad and Mom. My aunt and uncle were there to care for us. People brought food to our house. We were safe, but I felt afraid. Something was wrong.

I remember when my parents told me Grandma had died. I cried because it hurt. My grandma was so special. She made my favorite cookies and food every time we visited. She always smelled so good—like cinnamon, molasses, sugar, and cloves. I loved her hugs. I loved doing puzzles with her. Grandma was steady, calm, and love. She couldn't be dead. We just saw her and she was fine. I didn't understand. It hurt. And I cried.

I didn't attend her funeral either. The rest of my family did. I was left with some relatives in town, a place where I felt safe. However, I cried so hard that I almost made myself violently ill. I'm thankful for relatives who loved me and cared tenderly for me. But no one knew how confused I was about death. I cried, yes, but I didn't grieve. I didn't know how to grieve.

Instead, I wrapped up my pain, and buried it deep inside. It hurt too much.

Working with my counselor allowed me to unlock the grief buried deeply inside. Yes, I'd cried real tears in each situation. However, for me, those tears were simply a relief valve like the pressure valve on a pressure cooker. What I hadn't dealt with was the sudden loss, bewilderment, and irrevocable change in my life.

Each grief-causing situation involved a loss of a person, a dream, or a belief. Because I didn't know how, nor did I seek help from anyone else, I simply pushed away the feelings of loss. But the hole in my heart was still there. The wound covered over with a scab that kept leaking.

Once my counselor walked me back through the stages of grief[2] the wounds began to heal. It didn't change the fact that I desperately missed each person, but I simply learned how to walk the new path and enjoy life once again. More importantly, I discovered God's comfort. In one of my journaling sessions, this biblical passage jumped out:

*"As a mother comforts her child, so will I comfort you."*[3]

God was waiting for me to come to Him with my grief. He was willing to hear me express my pain which I did through journaling my questions, anger, and fears. As I wrote out each situation without filtering my thoughts, the chains of loss and bewilderment snapped away. Peace replaced the loss and bewilderment. Not all at once. But with each layer of grief I journaled through with God, He healed another piece of the wound.

Often I wished He'd just do the healing all at once. But that wasn't how it worked for me. Each counseling session, each journal entry revealed the next layer. Looking back, I can see God's mercy in this process. He alone understands what we can handle at any given time. In His unfailing love, He walks you and me through each layer when we are ready.

# When Healing Requires Remembering

*He heals the brokenhearted and binds up their wounds.*

Psalm 147:3

As the counselor and I continued to work through the grief process, once again the counselor walked me through a painful experience that I honestly thought I *had* grieved.

Days earlier I'd been to the doctor because I was sick again. Another round of bronchitis. The throaty coughs tore at my insides as if trying to rip my lungs from my rib cage. Treatment of my symptoms would be tricky this time due to my second pregnancy.

The doctor allowed me to go home under one condition: I had to stay in bed.

*"Yeah, right. How was I going to do that with a 10-month-old at home?"*

Nevertheless, the doctor was very firm, "Stay in bed or be hospitalized."

Dave drove me home after stopping to get the medication. I felt awful. Like I'd climbed the Empire State Building in lead boots with a mini-van strapped to my back.

*"What was I going to do?"*

Friends had offered to help with our 10-month-old, but this was going to involve larger blocks of time than any friend had, and the thought of orchestrating a gaggle of friends, lovely as they were, in and out of the house sounded too tiring. Not only did I need care for the baby, I also needed care for me.

Plus, I knew it was a major conference and event time for Dave. Long hours of work ahead and a sick wife at home. I glanced over at Dave and saw the stress lines etched in his face. The poor guy was tired. He didn't need me sick, again, on top of everything else.

"Do you think your mom could come and help out?" he quietly asked. "My parents are in Hawaii on vacation and I don't know how to reach them."

Just the thought of my mother's care brought joy. But, my dad had open-heart surgery only a few weeks ago. She couldn't leave him.

*"Could she? Could dad travel? Could I even ask her?"*

In desperation, I agreed to call my mom when we got home, once the long distance rates dropped for the evening. Living paycheck to paycheck, and now with more medical bills, I had to conserve money any way I could.

"Mom?"

With this one word, my mom knew something was wrong. She knew I was sick even though I was trying to sound as normal as possible.

"You don't sound good. What's wrong?"

"I have a severe case of bronchitis again. The doctor has ordered to me to stay in bed or he's going to put me in the hospital. I don't know what to do, Mom. I have a baby to care for, I can't stay in bed all day. And Daddy is still recovering from surgery so you can't come. I don't know what to do."

"Daddy's doing very well—remarkably well really. Let me talk with him and see what we can work out. I'll call you back in a bit. Just rest now."

A few hours later, the phone rang. My mother was coming the next day. She wondered if Dave could meet her at the airport. She'd stay as long as we needed her.

I was filled with relief, gratitude, and overwhelming guilt. On the one hand, I needed my mom. I don't care that I was a mother myself, expecting my second child. I needed my mom.

On the other hand, I was an adult, a wife, and a mother. I should be able to take care of my family. What was I doing running to mommy? My heart knew I wasn't really doing that, but the voices in my head shouted *"Failure. Weak. Sickie."* Over and over and over.

Did my dad need my mom more than I did? After all, my dad wasn't out of his critical recovery period after surgery. Mom's words rang in my head, "Dad said I had to come. No questions. You need me. He'll be fine. Your aunt will prepare his meals and they'll check on him every day. I'll call him daily as well. Plus other neighbors are here and will check on him every day. He'll be fine. I'll see you tomorrow. You rest now and stay in bed like the doctor ordered."

Relief ... and guilt warred within me.

*"Why was I so sick again? I'd been so careful not to be around those that were ill. I was getting enough rest. Yet I felt awful. Again."*

Mom arrived the next day and jumped right in to care for all of us. I was lying on the couch when she arrived, watching our daughter as best I could. Thankfully she was content to play near me. When Erin saw her Grandma, she lit up and crawled quickly, lifting her arms up to be held. Mom snapped her up and hugged her tightly, kissing her sweet face. Dave put Mom's suitcases away, while Mom fussed over Erin.

I awoke the next morning to hear my mom getting Erin up, changing her, and feeding her breakfast, Erin's sweet baby voice chattering happily away. Mom made sure Dave had time to get ready for work without the added burden of caring for Erin or me. Then, after Erin was settled with her toys, Mom prepared breakfast for me—a poached egg with toast, just like she did when I was a child. I was relieved and finally felt like I could rest, really rest. Mom would take care of everything once again.

The next day, Mom drove me to my OB appointment. I didn't feel good—kind of achy—but with the bronchitis I wasn't surprised. After my exam, the doctor said he wanted me to go to the hospital for an ultrasound. Said he wanted to check how the baby was doing. I'd never had an ultrasound before, so this was new and exciting.

During the ultrasound, the technician turned the screen and explained the image. Since the screen was at an awkward angle, it was hard to see what she was seeing. I did see the baby though because the technician pointed out the child to me. She remarked that it was interesting that the baby was being so calm. "Normally they scoot all over the place during an ultrasound. Don't like being invaded very much," she said. As with most technicians, she couldn't give me much information. The doctor would call me with a full report once he'd had time to view the ultrasound.

That night during dinner I didn't eat much. I was rather uncomfortable. In fact, I felt crampy. I mentioned how I was feeling to Dave and my mom. I wondered if this was just the bronchitis meds making me feel worse before I'd get better. But the cramps continued and then got stronger. Finally we decided to call the doctor. When I explained my symptoms to the triage nurse on the doctor's answering service, she advised we go to the hospital immediately. She'd contact the doctor and he'd meet me there.

# When There Were Two In The Moonlight

*"O God, listen to my cry! Hear my prayer! From the ends of the earth, I cry to you for help when my heart is overwhelmed."*

*Psalm 61:1-2 NLT*

Now I was scared.

*"What had I done? Had I somehow hurt my baby?"*

We left right away, thankful again that Mom was there with Erin. At least she would feel safe and be well loved. We promised to keep Mom updated after we got to the hospital.

The drive to the hospital seemed to take forever. Less than a mile from the hospital, the cramps were so severe I was breaking out in a sweat. I urged Dave to hurry. Something was terribly wrong. I knew it. I sensed it. And I was afraid. As we pulled into the emergency room parking lot, I was breathing hard from the pain and the fear combined. Dave stopped the car and ran around to help me get out of the car. As I stood up, I felt a gush. Dave scooped me up and ran through the emergency room doors.

The triage nurse heard us coming and said, "Fill out your name on the clipboard...." And then she saw me and the blood. Immediately, she yelled for a gurney and they rushed me back to a room.

Everything happened quickly—lots of medical staff and questions. I kept asking for my doctor.

Dave called our pastor. Somehow he got to the hospital in time to hear the ER doctor say they had to take me into emergency surgery. I was bleeding too heavily. I was losing the baby.

However, because I had eaten in the last hour, there was a real risk to the surgery. I could aspirate and die. Also, I had bronchitis, another complication. They'd do everything they could to prevent the aspiration and they'd monitor my breathing carefully, but we had to understand the risks.

I was losing my baby. And I was bleeding heavily. I had to have the surgery.

I was losing my baby.

Dave held me close, told me how much he loved me. Our pastor prayed quickly as the medical team rushed me down the hall. I grasped Dave's hand as long as possible. And then held his eyes as long as I could even after the operating room doors started to swing closed.

"Father, please be with Dave. Please. Hold me, Father" is the last thing I remember.

The room is dark.

*"Where am I?"*

Cool mist irritates my nose. Overwhelmed with the sensation, I scratch at my face.

Everything feels like it's in slow motion.

*"Where am I?"*

Slowly, agonizingly, the fog creeps away. I turn my head as the blood pressure cuff begins its constriction. The beeping machine penetrates my senses.

A hospital room. Alone. Dark. Empty.

*"I feel empty. Why?"*

Too tired, my eyes drift closed as consciousness slips into troubled sleep.

I don't know how long before I wake again. But this time, I know where I am and why.

As my mind fog clears, my eyes fill and overflow.

*"No longer pregnant. My baby died in my womb."*

*"What had I done?"* The darkness now appropriate for my sorrow.

Quietly a nurse comes in to check my vitals. Sniffing quietly, I reach up to wipe the tears but can't do anything about the nose. It's no use. The tears are flowing too heavily. Keeping my head turned the other way in raw grief, I pray she'll do her job and leave.

*"Try not to make a whimper or sound of any kind,"* I tell myself.

The nurse quietly comes around the bed, "Are you in any pain?"

*"Just my heart,"* I think, while shaking my head slightly in response to her question.

"I'm sorry for your loss," she murmurs and then slips quietly through the door leaving me alone with my grief. Her tender ministrations further undo my waking emotions.

I turn toward the other side of the room and notice a shaft of light on the floor. With watery, anesthetized eyes I glance over to see the window coverings partly open. Moonlight floods the room as agonized sobs overwhelmed my fragile heart.

Staggering under the reality of my now empty womb, I feel no other pain.

*"My baby is gone."*

Assaulted by questions, I look again to the moonlight, toward the sky. Swift clouds tumble across, over, and under each other scurrying ahead of the blustery wind now hiding the moonlight. Skeletal tree limbs barely visible in the storm.

Suddenly, the clouds break open for just a moment revealing the full glory of the moon. Bright, almost defiant against the scudding clouds.

And then I see Him.

Jesus with His arms held toward His body as if shielding something from view.

Whispering, I ask, *"Jesus, is that my baby? Will You take care of my baby?"*

With utmost tenderness, He turns His body ever so slightly, lowers His arms, and I see a beautiful child nestled close to His heart.

Safe. Secure. Content. Whole.

"I'm holding your child and will never let go."

I knew my baby was safe.

But, like a climber readying for Everest, I carefully packed up my emotions and buried them deep in my heart. Life without my child would be an arduous climb. The pain was too intense to dwell on. I couldn't face it because I might never stop crying. Besides, a good Christian knows that God is always good and always does what is best.

That is true. But it doesn't mean we can't grieve. Jesus grieved during His lifetime. At that time, I didn't understand that grief is part of life. I didn't know that burying my grief would only increase my pain.

I didn't know.
I didn't understand.
I didn't grieve.

I cried. But I didn't grieve.

# When Unresolved Issues Reveal The Darkness

*Relieve the troubles of my heart and free me from my anguish.*

Psalm 25:17

Through counseling I discovered the destructive consequences of burying my emotions all those years. Not only was I suffering from depression, but also unexplained physical ailments.

My body was reeling from the emotional trauma I'd stuffed behind my prison walls. I experienced several episodes of "heart attack" symptoms along with panic attacks, all of them mysteriously undetectable to physicians. Although they couldn't refute the physical symptoms I displayed, nothing was ever detected. I thought I was losing my mind.

A few months into my counseling, my fears became clear. My biggest fear was rejection—by Dave.

There's a picture I drew in my journal describing my awakening feelings. It is a close-up of me, overweight and holding a box of food, confused, with a broken heart, tears streaming down my face, my wedding rings dropping to the ground. Over my shoulder I see the open door of our house while Dave drives away. I've been rejected and abandoned.

A week later, I wrote:

> *"I feel disconnected, LORD, like I'm just going through the motions. It's almost like I'm simply checking things off a list to say I've done that. My emotions feel dead. I'm not really happy or sad or angry or excited. I'm just dead. Why? I can't seem to work my way through the fog. I'm just here in it. I don't feel anxious or worried either. I just don't think I'm feeling at all."*

Our first grandchild was due in less than a month. On Dave's birthday, just over a month after Erin & Casey's wedding, they told us they were expecting. A honeymoon pregnancy! While we were thrilled, they were still shocked. This baby was due before their first anniversary. A lot to process in their first year of marriage!

Our first granddaughter would be arriving soon! I'd lovingly created special gifts for this sweet one. But on the day of my daughter's baby shower, a day that should have been filled with joy, excitement, and expectation, my emotional world was gray.

My heart cried out with the Psalmist:

> *"LORD, don't hold back your tender mercies from me. Let your unfailing love and faithfulness always protect me. For*

*troubles surround me—too many to count! My sins pile
so high I can't see my way out. They outnumber the hairs
on my head. I have lost all courage. Please, LORD, rescue
me! Come quickly, LORD, and help me."*[1]

I was rapidly approaching the bottom of this pit, this prison
I'd climbed into. The darkness now so deep there was no
light. There was no tunnel with a light at the end.

It was pitch black dark. I could no longer pray because
my prayers didn't go any higher than the ceiling. I couldn't
read my Bible—it didn't make sense. I couldn't think more
than a word at a time. All I wanted to do was sleep. The
depression was engulfing my mind.

And I was lost.

During this time, as part of learning to be transparently
honest with a select few, I confessed this deadness first to
Dave and then to our Restoration Team. Dave began to
pray for me and over me—out loud. A great help because
I couldn't pray at all. It felt like my prayers ricocheted off
the ceiling to crumble onto the floor. Lifeless, like I felt.

Our faithful Team also covered us in prayer. Though that
was less tangible at the time, I knew they were praying and
was thankful.

Not only was I in an emotional crisis, I was in a spiritual
crisis. Everything I'd believed, or thought I'd believed, about
God suddenly wasn't believable. Questions bombarded me.
Lies slithered around my mind and heart. I couldn't discern
reality from sickness; truth from lies. I couldn't read my

Bible, except for the Psalms. The
ones that made the most sense
to me were those called the
Imprecatory Psalms. These are
psalms that call down curses or

> Depression is an ugly,
> often misunderstood,
> disease.

judgments upon the psalmist's enemies. Phrases like:

> *"break the teeth in their mouths"*[2]
> *"may all who gloat over my distress be put to shame and
> confusion"*[3]
> *"my heart is in anguish within me, the terrors of death
> have fallen on me"*[4]

Oh, the anger in my soul!

God used these psalms, that I consumed regularly, to break
down the strongholds in my heart. While these psalms call
down all sorts of retribution on the psalmist's enemies,
they also contain another common element: praise and
thanksgiving for who God is. Even in the midst of my most
depressed state, the Holy Spirit was speaking truth to me
about the character of my God. He was removing the gray
fog of spiritual confusion.

I hated looking at myself honestly. Hated it.

I hated the black, putrid, oozing sickness coming out of my
soul, mind, and heart. God was working as He promised.
But the surgical precision of His Holy Spirit revealed the
true depth of my pain.

Lies I'd believed for so many years, now exposed to the light, disgusted me. I didn't like who I was, who I'd allowed myself to become.

While depression was frightening, self-discovery was excruciating, intense, and revealed a much different image than I'd believed.

I came face to face with my sin as I dealt with the lies. I wrote,

> *"Lord, I want to be whole, not sick any longer. Clean out the putrid stench in my soul."*

And God answered my prayer.

# When The Answer Comes At The Bottom

*I waited patiently for the Lord; he turned to me and heard my cry. He lifted me out of the slimy pit, out of the mud and mire; he set my feet on a rock and gave me a firm place to stand.*

Psalm 40:1-2

The answer came at the bottom of the pit.

I remember the day I hit the bottom of the pit. I knew I was there because I had nothing left to argue about or to live for. I was done.

It was the blackest moment of my life, totally devoid of feeling. It just was. Emotionally I felt like a wedding dress blackened by pigsty mud and discarded in a heap. I smelled the rotten sludge. Unlovable. Rejected and abandoned. Utterly alone.

That's when I saw Him. My foggy eyes detected a small light off to my side. And there He was. Jesus. His arms open wide. Reaching toward filthy, crumpled, rejected me. He hadn't left me alone after all. He was there in the depths of the pit, the prison of my mind.

And I heard Him say, "Who do you believe I am?"

In that moment, I called His name, "Jesus." With stunning clarity, my decision became clear: Either my God was who He said He was or He wasn't.

If I chose to believe He wasn't, then my life was over. There was absolutely no reason to keep trying.

I had nothing left to give. Nothing more to try. Nothing that made sense in this mess outside of the grace of God.

It was in that moment that I chose to believe. I whispered, "Jesus, I believe. Help my unbelief."[1]

And Jesus wrapped His arms around me. For the first time in months, I felt safe. My feet suddenly on solid ground. The smell gone. I didn't soar to gleeful heights, as angels sang about me, but I found my feet. And that was high enough for me right then.

> I had nothing left to give. Nothing more to try. Nothing that made sense in this mess outside of the grace of God.

Recovery was now possible. I had HOPE.

Once I hit bottom, I almost felt relief. No more free-fall. Though it was just the beginning, I knew I was going to recover.

My choice involved identifying those thoughts that were false, the negative self-talk, and the lies I believed for so many years. If I hoped to recover, I needed to know the truth.

As the medication began to change my ability to sleep and think, cognitive thought returned. I was able to string two words together, followed eventually by sentences that made sense. A small victory.

I was learning to celebrate these victories. And as I celebrated them, hope increased.

## Dave

I hear stories of instantaneous healing from smoking, alcohol, drugs, and other addictive behaviors. I think, "Why, Lord, can't you do that for me?" The answer seems to be, "I could do that, but I'm choosing not to."

It's true that God could heal me immediately but there are lessons He wants me to learn in the process. Pornography is a struggle for many. And with internet access starting at younger and younger ages, it is becoming a problem for younger and younger people, mainly boys. Yes, God does heal instantaneously but a lot of times He chooses not to. I'm learning that I am healing, but it is a daily process.

I was learning any physical or emotional conditions could throw either of us into our personal addictions.

> "Simply going to bed on a regular schedule to get a good night's rest can help one's brain be more focused on positive habits and more alert to fight temptations. Not only eating but also eating well can improve mood and feelings of wellbeing. Regular exercise keeps the mind more focused, the body feeing great, and improves sleep."[2]

It became very important to take a daily pulse of our physical needs.

# The Covenant

# When Hurt Becomes Healing

*He put a new song in my mouth, a hymn of praise to our God. Many will see and fear the Lord and put their trust in him.*

Psalm 40:3

My contract job was up for renewal. While I was making progress in the counseling, I still had a long way to go.

Physically I wasn't doing well. It takes time to adjust to the medications used for depression. And, as is typical, we were still working through the right drug or drug combination that would provide the most assistance. There was some progress but I still wasn't sleeping well which exacerbated my exhaustion.

Dave was experiencing victory in his struggles through using accountability software on our computers, weekly connection with each of the men on our Team, and daily decisions to "bounce the eyes" (look away).

Each day, each hour, he had to make the decision for purity, to protect our marriage, and honor his vows. He'd completed the required six-month probationary period with his employer and met all their requirements. We were thankful he still had his job.

After talking through my job renewal options with each other and the Restoration Team, and praying for several weeks, we all came to the conclusion that it was better for our healing process and me if I opted not to renew the contract. I needed the extra time to work through the issues revealed in my counseling, to work on my physical health, and to invest in my marriage.

Mentally I finally felt like I was gaining ground. As the fog began to clear, thanks to the medication, problems worked themselves out more quickly. No longer did I struggle to solve the simplest issues such as balancing a checkbook. It's like my brain awakened a little bit more each day. My curiosity about life returned and along with it color. The world exploded in color—breathtaking, beautiful color.

Emotionally, we both struggled, because it is painstaking work to identify the false emotion and replace it with truth.

Counselor, Jenny Heckman defines emotional health as *"a combination of three facets: the ability to accurately identify the internal experience of our emotions; the ability to convey those feelings to another in ways that honor their dignity; and the ability to understand the emotional world of another."*[1]

I'd taught myself not to trust my emotions, to shut them off, now I needed to learn to recognize and acknowledge my emotions for what they were. I needed to accept the joy and the pain.

I learned that anger wasn't immoral. It was an emotion like any other and needed healthy expression.

I learned that disagreeing with my spouse wasn't wrong. It was, in fact, healthy when done in an honoring and respectful manner.

I learned it was good and right and healthy to care for myself before caring for others.

I learned that my big, loud laugh released tension in my soul. It was good.

I learned to cry with others, because I actually felt their pain. I didn't carry it, but I felt it. And it was good.

I learned that my need for quiet and alone time didn't have to mean I was depressed. It could mean I needed time to restore my soul the way the Father created me—in solitude.

I learned it was okay to ask for a hug when I needed it.

I learned that some days you aren't as upbeat as others and that's okay.

I learned I needed deep, heart connecting, truth-filled friendships with other women.

And when I did engage in those friendships I found I wasn't a pessimist after all. I was an optimist—a glass-half-full kind of woman. I delighted in sunrises and sunsets, new baby cuddles and sloppy toddler kisses, snow and rain and sunshine.

Dave also began to see his emotions in a new light. Emotions often signal an issue we need to address in the same way that a fever is the body's way of letting us know an infection is present. They are the alert language of the soul.

Dave learned to identify his emotions and recognize the triggers that were present so he could then search for the truth.

> Emotions are the alert language of the soul.

- Was he overly tired? Then it was time to slow down or take a nap or both.
- Was he angry? Why? What caused the anger and how could he constructively deal with it?
- Was he hurt? It was okay to express the cause of the hurt.
- Was he lonely? Reach out to me or another one of his accountability partners for some healthy human interaction.

## Dave

There were a couple of things, as I look back, that were triggers.

1. Feeling especially stressed at work
2. Feeling tired
3. Being bored

The HALT acronym—Hurt, Angry, Alone, and Tired—which I learned in counseling is a good reminder to stop when you're feeling any of those four emotions. When people feel any one of these four emotions they look for comfort. Sometimes they find comfort in an unhealthy way. Any one of those or several at the same time would trigger my hunger for pornography. Those were the times I found it the most difficult to stay away from the internet.

## Kirsten

We continued to work on our communication. Learning to communicate honestly without attacking each other in the process took daily practice. We failed often. Then we had to learn to admit our failure to the other, ask for forgiveness, and receive that forgiveness. When you've spent a lifetime beating yourself up for every mistake, you don't unlearn that thinking process easily. Learning to forgive yourself was as critical as forgiving the other person.

When you refuse to forgive yourself, you are in essence saying that God's forgiveness isn't enough.

*For as high as the heavens are above the earth, so great is his love for those who fear him; as far as the east is from the west, so far has he removed our transgressions from us.*[2]

> When you refuse to forgive yourself, you are saying that God's forgiveness isn't enough.

If God said that He forgave me, what made me think I had the right to not forgive myself? Every time Dave or I rehearsed our past sins, we demeaned God. This was deeply convicting and difficult to press into but necessary to encourage the growth of our feeble faith. But learning to live in the present, in forgiveness, meant leaving the past behind. Once the sin was confronted, it was time to accept God's forgiveness and move forward in the freshness of God's mercy and faithfulness.[3]

A particularly tough lesson for us to learn was that it is possible to love someone even though you may not like them at the moment. There were days when we struggled to get along. We'd snip at each other with minimal provocation. In these early days of restoration this felt monumental. It wasn't. Usually this scenario boiled down to one or both of us being selfish. Or, one had hurt the other in some way.

Through counseling, we learned techniques to remove the emotions from the moment. Statements like, "When you said that or did that, this is how I felt" taught us good, healthy communication. We learned it was healthy and good to confront less than desirable behavior. In Donald Miller's book, *Scary Close*, he states,

> "There's truth in the idea we're never going to be perfect in love but we can get close. And the closer we get, the healthier we will be. Love is not a game any of us can win, it's just a story we can live and enjoy."[4]

The more we learned to deal quickly with each other in these less than desirable moments, the healthier we became. And the less drama we created.

We had to learn to fight for our marriage and protect it at all costs. We had to learn what measures to take to build a supporting hedge around our marriage. One of the ways we did that was giving each other access to our personal email accounts. Dave could read my email at any time and I could read his.

Another protection we put in place was to not travel to a business meeting, such as a training event or conference, with a person of the opposite sex. Often that meant driving separately, if there were only two of us going to that particular event. Sometimes it also meant we had to deal with misunderstanding from business associates that thought we were being strict. It also meant no business lunches with only one person of the opposite sex.

When Dave traveled, he agreed to unplug the television in his hotel room. He told me of one incident when he was going to turn it on to check the weather, but to keep his word, he pulled up the information on his phone instead. He'd said no television, so that meant no television.

Another huge protection we added was computer accountability software on all internet accessible devices. Our every move on the internet was tracked on a weekly report sent to selected accountability partners. The first software we used was x3watch[5], a software that works on all platforms. Currently we use CovenantEyes[6], another accountability software, on all our internet accessible devices. The peace of mind we both feel with these services far outweighs the financial investment. We review the weekly reports together.

With nothing hidden, there is freedom. No reason to fear someone looking over your shoulder or in your historical internet searches.

# When Beauty Awakens

*The Lord has done great things for us, and we are*
*filled with joy.*

Psalm 126:3

While we were in Europe, we visited several castles. I was fascinated by the tapestries, some in better condition than others, but all intricately woven. Having done counted cross-stitch and needlepoint, I know that the front and back of a piece look very different. The back is a mass of tangled threads, and mismatched colors. It looks nothing like the magnificent artistry visible on the front.

All I'd been studying were the knots of my life.

God the Father now gave me a glimpse of the front of the tapestry of my life. Not the whole thing, but glimpses of the beauty He was creating.

A new tenderness for others.
A sense of peace I'd never experienced.
A desire to help others experience that peace.
A freedom to live authentically without looking around to make sure others approved of me.

A new understanding of who I am in Christ.
A grace to forgive myself for being human.

I learned the importance of forgiving others quickly and freely.

In several sessions, my counselor took me through some forgiveness exercises designed to identify hurts and then joys.

At each hurt, I had to answer the question, "Did Jesus' death pay for that hurt?"

The obvious answer to that question is "yes." But the underlying exercise forced me to consciously take that hurt to Jesus, lay it down at His feet, and ask Him to give me the ability to forgive. Each time I practiced this exercise a chain snapped away and my spirit lightened.

The second part of this exercise, was to list everything and everyone I was thankful for. At first, this was more difficult than remembering the hurt. But then it changed for me like the sun coming out from behind a cloud. When we begin to shift our minds to seek out that which is positive, we suddenly become more observant, more grateful, and more joyful. Throughout these sessions, my joy list grew significantly longer than my hurt list.

As my mind learned to focus on gratitude, the chains of guilt, shame, despair, retribution, and judgment began to snap like dry twigs.

*Therefore, since we have been justified through faith, we have peace with God through our Lord Jesus Christ, through whom we have gained access by faith into this grace in which we now stand. And we boast in the hope of the glory of God. Not only so, but we also glory in our sufferings, because we know that suffering produces perseverance; perseverance, character; and character, hope. And hope does not put us to shame, because God's love has been poured out into our hearts through the Holy Spirit, who has been given to us.[1]*

The old sinful, destructive patterns were revealed. The chains were snapping away. The door to my prison no longer securely shut.

God's Light penetrated my soul, which resulted in significant healing. On Dave's next business trip, I actually flirted with him via text message and phone messages. Plus, I missed him desperately, which was another indicator of my inner healing. I couldn't wait to see his handsome face again. I hungered for intimacy with him.

After being in the depths of depression, I was so thankful for the renewing of my mind. It was wonderful to be able to pray again and know that God, my Father, was listening and answering.

# When You Are Completely Known And Fully Loved

*Therefore, as God's chosen people, holy and dearly loved, clothe yourselves with compassion, kindness, humility, gentleness and patience. Bear with each other and forgive one another if any of you has a grievance against someone. Forgive as the Lord forgave you.*

*Colossians 3:12-13*

I wrote in my journal at the beginning of 2009,

*"How much God has grown me up in the last year. In many ways, I feel like a child who is learning to walk; in some ways I feel old and bruised and battered."*

Two contrasting feelings. Two realities in harmony. No longer stuck in a childhood memory, either one of us.

In the past 18 months, we'd begun the process of identifying our fears. We'd learned to remove the masks. We'd peeled back the layers covering our real selves. We'd discovered the freedom[1] that comes from bringing everything into the light. As the Bible says, we were no longer condemned[2], no longer bound in the prison of lies.

The restoration process revealed that there were safe people in this world. This group knew all about Dave and me. We'd left no part of our lives hidden. They'd asked every question you can imagine. They'd met with our marriage counselor receiving access to his evaluation of us. We'd given them permission to enter every area of our life.

And they'd proven they were safe.

They loved us, nurtured us, corrected us, supported us, protected us, and now brought us to a place of being fit for ministry once again. They'd walked us through the worst of the battle. They helped to heal our wounds. They were "Jesus with skin on," totally trustworthy. We were completely known and fully loved in a way we'd never experienced before.

Yet, on that January day, when we met with our Restoration Team, along with our children, to be released from their oversight, I had mixed emotions.

It was a momentous day. It was a day of celebration, thanksgiving, and gratefulness. It was also an unnerving day, which surprised us.

The Team spoke with our kids first, willingly answering any questions they had about our restoration process. The Team's tenderness with our children brought tears, real tears, of joy and gratefulness.

No longer in the gray, I felt the full range of emotions. I was awake for the first time in years.

Then, we each had time to speak to our children. Throughout this whole ordeal, our kids' maturity, grace, and love ministered to our brokenness. We feebly attempted to communicate how they blessed us. By this time, our youngest son was home again. I was so thankful Nate was part of this special day.

Our Team then spoke to Dave and me as a couple and as individuals. While the formal times together as a Team were ending, it didn't mean they were stepping out of our lives. They would be available to us whenever we needed them. I, for one, was thrilled to hear this. Because I knew that even though we had done the hard work and met the criteria for restoration, I knew my deceitful heart.[3]

Frankly, I was scared to be "set free." I didn't trust myself. I was still learning to trust Dave and God. I felt like a baby who'd just learned to stand up and take her first steps. The Father was a long way across the room calling me to come to Him. The distance was enormous! And I wasn't sure I could get there. I was sure I'd fall flat on my face in just a few steps.

For the last 18 months, this Team had literally controlled our lives. They created a protective cocoon which allowed us to heal, mature, and change within a warm, safe environment. I seriously doubted whether I had matured enough, worked through enough of the issues, and trusted Dave enough to walk this new path without the safety net.

It was in that moment, that I first began to truly run to God with my questions and fears. Yes, I still had fears. Yes, I still heard those lies being whispered in my ears. Yes, I still had the same temptations. I prayed I would recognize them better and call them what they were.

I wrote in my journal, a discipline I now realized helped me focus my thoughts and prayers,

> *"Will I be strong enough to understand what is [the Father's] best and not just do or decide on what is expedient or expected? Have I learned to trust You, Father, enough to wait for Your leading? I don't want to go back into hiding my real self. Father, please help me to trust You enough to be real with others. To not be stupidly transparent, but to be the person You created me to be regardless of what people think of me."*

The door to my prison was now thrown open wide. The choice before me:

Walk through the door into freedom and light?
Or
Step back into the shadows and fear.

With trembling breath and shaking feet, I took that first step. For the first time in a lifetime, I breathed in the fresh air.

# When You Choose
# To Begin Again

*"The beauty of the covenant-keeping love between Christ and his church shines brightest when nothing but Christ can sustain it."*

John and Noël Piper

We were two broken, messed up people beginning to learn the meaning of covenant.

The dance began anew. We stepped on each other's toes a lot. I guess I thought that when I'd worked through the counseling, when we worked through the counseling, we would move past the consequences of our dysfunctional relationship.

I was wrong! Time to step away from that fairy tale—again!

The fairy tale says, "And they lived happily ever after!" The curtain closes. We all leave the theater feeling good with our "happily ever after" belief system.

Imagine everyone's shock when reality is something entirely different.

Thankfully, our Restoration Team continued to be a vital part of our lives. They were faithful to check in with us regularly. But the hard work of living life in covenant with each other could only be done by us.

Jerry Sittser, in his book *A Grace Revealed*, wrote

> *"Redemption is the work of Jesus Christ applied to the unfolding story of life, your life and my life...Redemption happens through God's involvement in the ordinary circumstances of life, no matter what those circumstances happen to be."[1]*

Learning to walk together in redemption, in covenant, was humbling. No longer did I want to live in the prison of lies I'd created. What our Restoration Team said early on was true. My perfect world didn't exist.

Dealing with your sin, the lies and fears you've held for so long as truth, is a monumental struggle. For some reason, we humans tend to classify sin. Perhaps we do this to justify our actions. Perhaps it is our drive to look good in someone's eyes. Maybe it's our insecurities or personal lack of self-worth. Maybe it comes from a place of deep woundedness. Maybe it's simply part of the sin nature we're all cursed with since Adam and Eve sinned in the Garden of Eden.

The truth is sin is sin. Period. No classifications. Everything contrary to the nature of God is sin.

| | |
|---|---|
| Dishonesty | Gossip |
| Idolatry | Lying |
| Taking God's name in vain | Cheating |

Lust

Covetousness

Breaking a vow

Dishonoring parents

Adultery

Pride

Fornication

Holding a grudge

Unkind words

Murder

Stealing

Haughty eyes

False testimony

Scheming to harm another

Troublemaking

Turning a blind eye to evil

Not willing to work to support yourself

Accepting a bribe

Bribery

Slander

Usury

Piling up debt with no intention to pay

Showing no respect for another's life

Gluttony

Selfishness

Arrogance

Hatred

Jealousy

Impurity

Witchcraft

Fits of rage

Dissension

Envy

Drunkenness

Pornography

Conceit

Malice

Abandonment

The list of sins is endless.

Yet nowhere does the Bible say that one of these sins is greater than another. All are sin. All break fellowship between you and another. More importantly, all break your relationship with the Father.

> "Why do you look at the speck of sawdust in your brother's eye and pay no attention to the plank in your own eye?"[2]

I wanted to believe that Dave's pornography addiction was so much worse than my sin. But the truth is, it wasn't.

We were in this desperate situation because we both were living a lie. Neither one was being truthful with ourselves or with each other. By focusing on Dave's sin, I justified ignoring my own. I deceived myself that the prison I frequented wasn't a prison at all.

However, it wasn't, and isn't, possible to change another person. The only person I could change was me. My behaviors, attitudes, and words were my responsibility. Not Dave's. He was responsible for himself. Not me. When Dave and I began to grasp this reality, the temperature in our marriage changed.

> The only way our marriage would survive was if we both turned first toward God for healing, forgiveness, and restoration, and then toward each other in complete submission.

The truth is we were more concerned about preserving our self-image than living authentically. We were more worried about what each other thought than what the Father thought. I learned to pray for my husband every day. I learned to praise the Father for my husband every day. I learned to focus on my husband's goodness and love for me.

We had allowed sin to invade and permeate our hearts and minds to the point that we became comfortable. No longer staying as far away from the lie as possible, we were willingly and eagerly climbing into our individual prisons to camp out or explore their depths.

And in that exploration we found captivity and pain. Not the sense of acceptance we longed for. No rise in respect. Instead, we walked in constant fear of being revealed, always looking over our shoulder to make sure our real selves weren't discovered. We rationalized our lack of integrity.

The sense of "if people really knew who I was they'd reject me" grew every day.

The turning point came when I fully grasped the depth of my sin, when I quit placing blame at Dave's feet, and accepted my responsibility for my actions, my sin, and my woundedness.

The only way our marriage would survive was if we both turned first toward God for healing, forgiveness, and restoration, and then toward each other in complete submission.

**We were both at fault for the status of our marriage.**

**We would only survive by fighting for our marriage.**

> *"You see it's not always 50/50 in marriage. Sometimes it's 80/20 or 100/0 but when you understand that, you are more willing to take your turn because there will come a day when you need to be the one held up instead. The greatest battles couples are going to face in marriage aren't with each other but for each other."[3]*

And so we began.

# When You Realize Covenant Is More Than A Contract

> "When the impossible day comes that Christ breaks his vow, 'I am with you always, to the end of the age,' then, on that day, a human being may break his marriage covenant."
>
> John and Noël Piper

W hen our world fell apart almost a decade ago, the question we both had to answer was, "Would our marriage survive? Would we stick it out?"

The night Dave told me of his pornography addiction, I recall him asking me if he should sleep on the couch. I believe my answer at that time was God-ordained. Even in my confusion and pain, the Holy Spirit was reminding me of my covenant.

> "A covenant is intended by God to be a lifelong fruitful relationship between a man and a woman. Marriage is a vow to God, to each other, our families, and our community to remain steadfast in unconditional love, reconciliation and

*sexual purity, while purposefully growing in our covenant marriage relationship."*[1]

Later, when confronted by the Lord about my vows, the marriage covenant finally hit home. This was not a contract that could be broken because I was deeply hurt and uncomfortable. This was a covenant made not just with Dave, but with God. It was binding. At the time I made it, I had no idea how serious it was.

The Scripture passage that I used to pretend I had an out,

> *"But I tell you that anyone who divorces his wife, except for sexual immorality, makes her the victim of adultery, and anyone who marries a divorced woman commits adultery"*,[2]

Jesus said, was allowed by Moses because Israel's people were stubborn and hard-hearted. It was not that way in the beginning.[3]

God said that when a man and woman marry they become one flesh. One flesh. In the eyes of God. Not only that, but Jesus said marriage is a picture of His love for His followers.[4] Marriage is a covenant between three people: the groom, the bride, and God.

Merriam-Webster Dictionary defines covenant as "a usually formal, solemn, and binding agreement."

Sounds a lot like a contract. Contract means "a binding agreement between two or more persons or parties; legally binding."

Contract, which can be certified by a handshake or a signature, usually means I'm protecting my rights in case something in this relationship goes sour.

When you dig deeper into the meaning of covenant, it usually involves some sort of an oath, which means you are bound by your words to fulfill the covenant. No matter what, it involves carrying through to the benefit of another. It is other-focused instead of self-protective.

> "Marriage has a unique place because it speaks of an absolute faithfulness, a covenant between radically different persons, male and female; and so it echoes the absolute covenant of God with his chosen, a covenant between radically different partners." Rowan Williams

In this covenant, we'd said, "Until death do us part." Since we were both still very much alive, we had to confront the terms of our covenant.

Our new reality proved we didn't understand the depths of covenant. By this time we were getting a clue, but reality was more difficult than we'd imagined.

While we *said* our marriage was important, we had to *learn* to put our relationship ahead of other relationships.

We learned that first we had to be in right relationship with the Father, which included praying daily that He would change me, while also growing the other into the person He designed them to be. No longer begging, "Lord, change him(her)!" Our prayers became, "Lord, change me so I can love him/her with your love." The Father answers that prayer every day. We also began to pray with each other. It's true that you cannot be angry with someone with whom, and for whom, you are praying.

When we put our marriage relationship ahead of all others, it necessitated that some relationships had to dwindle or be cut off. Sometimes you have friendships outside your marriage that do not encourage your marriage. These types of "friendships" are toxic to you and your marriage.

Spending time with others who speak negatively of their spouse in public are not people who encourage your marriage. I remember being at lunch with a woman whose conversation was a steady diatribe of her husband's faults. At the end of that lunch, which I barely ate, I felt dirty, discouraged, and depressed. Even though I made several attempts to turn the conversation toward more positive comments, the litany of faults continued. I never met with that woman again. I didn't need her negativity toward her husband influencing me.

If you are friends with a person of the opposite sex, and you find yourself talking about your marriage problems to that person or giving them information you should only be telling your spouse, that relationship is inappropriate. You have pledged to share your heart with only one. To protect your marriage, this relationship must be let go. Dennis and Barbara Rainey, Christian authors married since 1972, explain it this way:

> "Emotional adultery is unfaithfulness of the heart. It starts
> when two people of the opposite sex [who aren't married]

*begin talking with each other about intimate struggles, doubts, or feelings. They start sharing their souls in a way that God intended exclusively for the marriage relationship. Emotional adultery is friendship with the opposite sex that goes too far."[5]*

We both had to evaluate our friendships and remove those that didn't fit our "new" relationship's paradigm. We needed to protect our marriage above all else.

We also had to correctly prioritize our marriage relationship with our other relationships. When you marry, you leave your family of origin and begin a new family. Consequently, the husband and wife relationship is now the primary one after the relationship with God. Without realizing it, other good relationships in our life—father, mother, children, or siblings—were not in their proper place. We had to decide and act on a new priority of God first, marriage next, children third, all other family fourth, and then everyone else. Even today, whenever we allow the relationship priorities to get in the wrong order we have problems.

By this time, we knew our marriage would survive. I knew I deeply loved this man. The Father had restored my love. And Dave loved me deeply. So, we began to date again.

Like many marriages, we'd let go of the art of dating. We'd forgotten how to flirt with each other. Through the normal pressures of life, we'd neglected playing together. Now we spent more time talking with each other, and more importantly listening. This was part of our daily discipline.

As he opened his heart to me, my love increased for this special man.

God the Father knew exactly whom I needed as a life partner. I'd always believed that before my world was shaken. Now I deeply knew, without a doubt, that this humble man was my best friend, lover, and partner in all things. He had my back always. He loved me completely. He would give his life for me.

But, my biggest struggle continued to be trust.

# When You Learn To Take Him At His Word

*We delight in the beauty of the butterfly, but rarely admit the changes it has gone through to achieve that beauty.*

*Maya Angelou*

When we were rearing our children, we taught them, "Trust is hard-earned and easily lost." Amazing how easy it is to say something like that, but to live it is something else entirely.

I desperately wanted to trust Dave, but I found myself questioning him every time he left for a business trip. It was too easy to fall into "mother" mode and grill him like I did one of my children when they were naughty. Even though we had agreed, with our Restoration Team, on the business travel parameters that Dave adhered to, I still struggled to trust him.

On the wise counsel of our Team, we agreed that I wouldn't be his main accountability partner. It was best that the men on our Team did that.

To keep me out of "mother" mode and remain in "wife" mode, we agreed on questions I would ask at any time.

- How are you doing today? - An open-ended question that he knew referred to his state of purity
- How are we doing? - Permission for him to tell me if there was anything in our relationship we needed to discuss

It seemed the Bible passages that referred to a nagging wife[1] would jump off the page during this time. It was too easy to slice and dice Dave with my words. I was learning what it meant to pray for my husband and let the Holy Spirit do His work without my interference.

Ultimately, the trust issue with Dave was rooted in my trust of God. Perhaps the most destructive lie I'd believed for so many years was that I couldn't fully trust the Father with my entire life.

Sure, I gave lip service to trusting God—with the big stuff like keeping the universe in place, natural disasters, that sort of thing—but when it came to my daily life I wasn't sure I could trust Him. I believed God was real but could I trust Him with my life?

The Bible says to cast my anxieties[2] on Him because He cares about me. It also says that not only could I bring my concerns to Him but also He would sustain me.[3] Thus, I began the slow process of learning to trust God as well as trusting Him with my husband.

Dave had to overcome this addiction in his own way and with God's help. While I could encourage him, I couldn't dictate how he did it. I could pray for him but I had to let God work in Dave *without my interference.*

And I had to respect my husband. I had to stop second guessing everything he told me and take him at his word. Therefore, I had to bring my cares and concerns to the Father. I had to ask the Holy Spirit to give me the ability to believe Dave. I had to ask forgiveness for my judgmental attitude about Dave's addiction. I had to agree with the Father that sin is sin.

I took small steps when I wanted to leap. Faltering steps. Often falling and skinning my knees. But each step was a step in my recovery from depression, a step toward building a stronger marriage, and a lesson in trust. And, in the midst of these steps, I began to understand the gift of grace.

I wrote in my journal on June 26, 2008:

> *"I don't want this statement '[she] refused to turn...' to be my legacy."*

> *But Jehu did not obey the Law of the LORD, the God of Israel, with all his heart. He refused to turn from the sins that Jeroboam had led Israel to commit.*[4]

While reading this passage that day, I was struck by Jehu's faithfulness to carry out God's command. Mostly. *But he was half-hearted and therefore his legacy was tainted.* The last significant thing written about Jehu was that *he refused to turn from the sins [of] Jeroboam.*

This was not the legacy I desired. Becoming fully alive and willing to turn renewed the sense of purpose for my life.

The process the Father had taken us through revealed our sins and failures. It was all too easy to get caught up in those failures.

I'd reared my children while being suicidally depressed. *"How much damage had I done to my children?"* Shame and guilt worked overtime to condemn me.

But the Father lovingly spoke Truth over me. He told me in Psalm 103 that He had removed my sins as far as the east is from the west. He reminded me that He loves my children more than I could possibly love them.

After all, my Father is also their Father. He would restore the years[5] of depression. He would make me stand strong in His Truth.

Through counseling I began to redefine my legacy. I learned to forgive myself, first. In one particular counseling session, we went through an exercise where I filled a large "pain egg" with smaller eggs named with the things that filled me with shame, hurt, or embarrassment.

In order to change my legacy, which I learned was possible, I had to look at each of these hurtful "eggs" and identify the lie. Then, I had to let go of the egg. I had to intentionally give up my desire and need to justify myself or my actions. This was not simple. It was in fact something that I worked through in my journals over the next few months. In the process, I developed a strong habit of *writing down* what hurt instead of *talking indiscriminately* about it.

> The Holy Spirit convicts in order to restore relationship and make us useful to the world. The enemy of our soul condemns in order to destroy us and to keep us from seeing our value.

My journaling now morphed into more of a conversation with God about the events of my life and how I actually felt about them. It was a safe place to be completely authentic. In the process of writing out the problem or pain I learned to stay in this place of written prayer until God's peace flooded my mind, heart, and soul. I learned to hear God speaking to me, usually through Scripture verses that came to mind.

I learned that the only way to combat a lie is to discover God's truth and apply it to the situation. The Holy Spirit convicts in order to restore relationship and make us useful to the world. The enemy of our soul condemns in order to destroy us and to keep us from seeing our value.

Those condemning voices I'd been hearing for so many years were the enemy. I learned to speak out loud against those voices, reciting Scripture verses that told me who I am in Christ.[6]

# When Your Trust Is Tested

*Those who know your name trust in you, for you, LORD,
have never forsaken those who seek you.*

*Psalm 9:10*

One of the hardest lessons is learning that trust is not a right. Just because you live with someone in marriage doesn't mean you trust that person. It is not a given.

I found that learning to trust Dave again was very difficult. But even more surprising was that I needed to learn to trust God first. And as I learned to trust God, I learned to trust Dave.

Through the counseling, I realized I didn't know what it meant to trust God with EVERYTHING. I sure talked about trusting God all the time. But I wasn't practicing it. I'd placed God in a box—a very small, comfortable, controllable box. And God refused to stay in it.

Instead, I continually bumped up against trust issues, such as my husband's travel schedule. One of hardest tests of my trust muscle came a few years later when Dave was downsized from his job. I'll never forget that day:

Brrrrng.

"You'll never guess what happened," Dave said. His next words took my breath away.

"I no longer have a job."

Six words.

*"What? How could this be? Without warning? Surely he's joking. He's gotta be."*

Dave decided to come home shortly. After all, he no longer had a job.

I must admit I wondered if he'd been looking at pornography again at work. He assured me that wasn't the reason. However, both of us wondered if the pornography addiction had any part in the decision to eliminate his job.

That day drudged up so many fears for both of us:

## Kirsten

*"Are we going to be pushed to the brink of financial failure? What if we lose our house? Who will hire us at our age?"*

## Dave

"Guess this means I'm not very good at my job after all."

242

Wave after wave of fears and lies flooded in. It was amazing how quickly fear tried to drag us down to its murky depths. But we didn't let it. We decided to practice what we'd learned the last few years—to take our thoughts captive.[1] Eventually, we both felt tremendous peace. It was astonishing!

By this time we had both learned (the hard way) that we could trust God with everything. Everything. He hadn't abandoned us before. Therefore, He wouldn't abandon us now. And He was bigger than this obstacle. Way bigger.

Don't get me wrong. This was not a comfortable, easy, relaxed time. We were both stunned. Fear attempted to take over our minds once again. But we made the decision to stop and pray first. And pray some more until our hearts were at peace.

And God met our specific need once again. We never once missed a mortgage payment or any other expense. We did curtail our spending down to the basics. We did our due diligence in searching for work. We trusted God to provide for all our needs and He did. Every. Single. Time.

I've thought back on the timing of this event many times. God had prepared my heart, and Dave's, far ahead of time.

God had proven Himself faithful in the restoration of our marriage. We could trust Him to provide once again. And He did. Within a few short months, Dave accepted a job. While no job is perfect, this job allowed him to provide for our family and pursue some new dreams professionally and personally.

A bigger confirmation of my personal restoration was the confidence I had in Dave. I knew beyond a shadow of a doubt that he would do everything he could to financially provide for our family. I realized I did trust him because I never doubted what he was telling me.

We talked through our personal fears honestly and openly. We called our Team for prayer support, and got job search guidance as an additional bonus. We knew we had a community, including our grown children, who supported us wholeheartedly. We prayed for each other and with each other. We discussed our options and brainstormed together. We had each other's back. We were not alone. We were not drifting. We didn't have all the answers but we could identify the next step, one day at a time.

# When You Choose Integrity

*The weapons we fight with are not the weapons of the world. On the contrary, they have divine power to demolish strongholds. We demolish arguments and every pretension that sets itself up against the knowledge of God, and we take captive every thought to make it obedient to Christ.*

2 Corinthians 10:4-5

Life wasn't perfect, but it was very, very good. My husband was the man I'd always believed him to be. He wasn't perfect, and neither was I. And I was grateful. Who'd want to be married to a perfect man?!

By taking off my blinders filled with false expectations, I set us both free to be who we were created to be.

In Dave's words, he desires to be a man of integrity. And he is.

## Dave

My desire is to get to the point where I deeply hate pornography. As Dr. Doug Weiss says, "You will never destroy an enemy you embrace."[1] Right now I do hate pornography because of what it does to my relationship with the Lord. Spiritually, when I turn to porn, I feel like the needle valve of a pump being put into a ball and deflating it. Totally flat, completely deflated, because the relationship is grieved. God hasn't turned away, He's still there. I've turned away.

It goes back to the shame when Adam and Eve covered themselves the Garden of Eden. Because of the shame I'm going to cover myself because I'm naked and ashamed. Then God says, "Who said you were naked? I never told you that." He doesn't love me less, but I hide my heart in fear.

I hate what pornography does to my relationship with God.

I hate what it does to my marriage relationship. It makes me ashamed to be around Kirsten, ashamed of leading a double life. I hate pornography, but I want to grow to hate it even more.

In Dave Carder's book, Torn Asunder, he says,

> "If you are going to live together in harmony in the future, you need to live together differently. It's time to start over.... The most sacred aspects of this marriage have already been violated. Now you both have to begin to rebuild.[2]

I need to live differently.

It's like Kirsten's hyper-sensitivity to cigarette smoke. It doesn't take much for her to sense cigarette smoke and feel the pressure in her lungs. It's the same for me on the internet. A tiny bit feels like too much.

I'm extremely careful on the internet now because I've got the accountability tracking software on there. But even beyond that, I don't know what image or what word or suggestion might trigger the pornography shame cycle. I'm trying to be extremely careful, to stay as far away from the temptation as possible.

Nowadays we track my online actions. I'm thankful for the tracking software on my computer because I can't hide from it. If it's the fear of getting caught, I'm fine with that!

That's a healthy fear for me. My phone is also tracked.

I know my actions are not hidden. And if I'm a "believer" that was never true before either. God knows my inner most thoughts.

Even searches that might appear innocuous could raise a red flag and I'd rather not do that. It's good accountability because I know one of my accountability partners can ask me about anything that appears on the weekly report.

But I'm encouraged now.

These days I'm actually seeing some progress. Instead of jumping in the cesspool, swimming around, enjoying a little garbage, and then jumping out, I'm staying as far away as possible. I'm trying to smell the stink before I get close.

I'm working to take every thought captive, to purify my mind. The accountability does help on all those levels.

## Kirsten

I want to be a woman of integrity as well. Part of living a life of integrity is admitting when you mess up. We're both learning this truth.

Integrity involves every area of your life.

Webster defines integrity as: "The quality or state of being complete; unbroken condition; wholeness; entirety."

Entirety.

A person of integrity is the same person wherever they are. You don't have to wonder which person you will talk with depending on the situation. Mark Twain said it this way, "If you tell the truth, you don't have to remember anything."

A person of integrity is truthful always, in every way, and every aspect of their life. I want to be that person.

# When You Choose
# The Open Door

*I waited patiently for the Lord; he turned to me and heard my cry. He lifted me out of the slimy pit, out of the mud and mire; he set my feet on a rock and gave me a firm place to stand. He put a new song in my mouth, a hymn of praise to our God.*

*Psalm 40:1-3*

I'll never forget the day when I finally felt free of the dark cloud of depression. What joy! What unbelievable peace! I remember waking up that morning with a sense of anticipation. It was a new day! A brand new day. I was alive and filled with wonder at what this day would bring.

My prison walls were coming down one stone at a time. The light penetrated the darkness with cleansing hope.

He answered my prayer for deliverance from the fog of depression.

He answered my prayer for restoration of my marriage.

He answered my prayer for a new and deeper love for my husband.

He answered my prayer for healing for my husband.

He removed me from the grayness and brought me into His colorful light.

Each step forward out of the prison of lies brought new breath, new joy.

God had taken Dave and me from our prison of lies to His restoration. We began to see new opportunities, something we never anticipated. And it was good. We continued to meet with members of our Restoration Team periodically. There had been setbacks for both of us, but we identified the triggers, healed, and moved forward much more quickly, no longer derailed by the lies of the past.

Our work with a business coach and mentor encouraged us to pursue passions we'd long buried. Now we had the trust in God and in each other that we could walk confidently in our dreams. We still didn't have all the specifics to make this happen, but we knew we could trust God enough to take the next step and the next and the next.

However, despite all the counseling, tools, Team, and victories over the last six years, I still struggled. The dark cloud was gone, but I felt agitated. Imagine a caged lioness at a zoo. Watch her pace back and forth watching you watch her. You can feel her intense desire for freedom. That's how I felt. I could smell it, almost taste it, but I couldn't break through to run free.

One night, while enjoying a beautiful summer evening on our deck, I blurted out my confusion and frustration at the "barrier" still in front of me. I believed I knew my purpose and passion, but still couldn't move forward. Something was holding me back but I couldn't identify it. We talked about this for a while, rejoicing in the progress we'd made in the last years. Life was really, really good. What was holding me back?

Without my prompting, Dave said, "I think you need to go to 'Escaping Shawshank'."[1] I was stunned and relieved. I'd been praying about attending this intensive coaching, which included time spent in a prison cell, for almost a month.

Though I wanted Dave to attend with me, it simply wasn't possible due to work commitments. Hindsight always reveals what we can't see in the moment. Though attending on my own wasn't what I'd been praying for, it was what God intended. I had no idea the significant resistance I would face simply to get to the event.

American author, Steven Pressfield has this to say about resistance,

> Resistance's goal is not to wound or disable. Resistance aims to kill. Its target is the epicenter of our being: our genius, our soul, the unique and priceless gift we were put on this earth to give and that no one else has but us. Resistance means business when we fight it, we are in a war to the death.[2]

The fight with resistance began as soon as I arrived at the airport. However, my step of faith to attend on my own, broke through that resistance. Here are my journaled thoughts as I sat in the cold, dank cell at the Ohio State Reformatory during my Escaping Shawshank experience.

*I sit here, my senses on overload, and wonder.*

*What brought me to this place of shame? Why am I here?*

*I see nothing beyond the bars and the brick wall. I move my head to try to look beyond the bars but I can't. They are constantly there.*

*Slowly I reach toward the bars, hesitant yet curious to feel them.*

*"Maybe if I get close enough."*

*Cold. Unyielding. Intimidating. There's a strange dank smell about them.*

*The bars are impressive, solid steel too large for me to fully grasp. I have an overwhelming impulse to shake them. I don't. I stand there with my face as close as possible. Immobile. Stunned.*

*As I step back I realize I can touch the wall on both sides. Turning around I peer at the grimy sink and toilet. Disgusting.*

*Afraid to step out of the small patch of light, I slide down the cold unyielding wall to the steel floor. My senses overwhelmed with deafening silence.*

*A helicopter. A sniffle. Faint murmurs. Sounds disconnected from anything real at the moment.*

*Another glance toward the light and the bars reveal a thick, heavy chain. Ominous. Short. Dangling there. How could something so still vibrate with such intensity? I hold my breath.*

*I don't want to know the strength of that chain, don't want to touch it. Somehow it seems more threatening than the steel bars. I feel it reaching toward me, willing me to stay deeply bound in this prison.*

*Questions tumble in my head, "What does it feel like to be chained? Is it another level of cruel restraint brought on by my behavior? Can I change my behavior now? Will I ever break free? Does it attach to a wrist or an ankle? Did I choose this? Will it cut me, and if it does will I bleed when I feel so dry inside? Why am I here?"*

*With a will of its own, my arm reaches toward the chain and I touch it. I imagine what it feels like to be bound. Unable to move more than a few feet from those hideous bars, no matter how I twist my restricted body, the heavy weight of the chain causes chronic pain in my arm. Pain I've felt for a year. It makes it difficult to lie down to rest. The floor is cold—unaware of my discomfort.*

*Perhaps that chain is just another level of security for these bars. Is it to secure the door? Is it protecting me?*

*Why the chain? Why these prison walls?*

*I realize I've wrapped my chain around my mind and emotions. I've built this prison. I've become comfortable with my chain like a childhood blanket. But this new chain threatens me. It isn't comfortable. It hurts. It is suffocating me. My heart begins to palpitate while my breathing quickens.*

*No longer hidden, my prison walls are exposed.*

*I built this prison, wire by wire, brick by brick. I carefully crafted the corners, secure but with enough bend that they wouldn't bruise too badly when I crashed into them. When the prison became too small, I pushed it further back, enlarged it to reach into the shadows where I believed I'd find protection. After a while, I found ways to cover the back end of that prison to hide me from others' unkind words or deeds.*

*The crazy thing was ... I had the key to the chain and the prison. I'd always had it. Yet, I continued to live there, to wear the chain with pride. I spent enormous effort gilding this prison to make it more comfortable, less like a prison. I wanted to feel cozy if I was going to live here.*

*There were whispers throughout the years that peaked my curiosity. Whispers that drew me closer to the door. Whispers that hinted at something better. Yet, as I crawled closer to the door light splashed over me, and I'd scurry back into the darkness, the power of the light more frightening than anything else.*

*What if someone saw me as I really am?*
*What if I get hurt again?*
*What if they reject me?*
*What if I fail?*
*What if I my words reveal how little I know?*
*What if I'm not funny enough?*

*All these questions bombarded me, the prospect of the true answers seemed worse than hiding. Besides, I was safe here in this prison.*

*Right?*

*This was my experience as I voluntarily walked into a prison cell in Ohio for a time of deep reflection and learning.*

*The Ohio State Reformatory[3] was built in the 1800's to be a reformatory for boys under the age of 18 that committed a petty crime. No hardened criminals, no "lifers". There was rehabilitation hope for these boys, which was the ultimate goal.*

*The Reformatory is built to look like a castle, an imposing, but beautiful sight. But around back, as I entered through the bullpen, I saw steel bars. Steel steps. Steel cells stacked up to six stories high. Steel upon steel everywhere I looked.*

*Our guide took us through the prison portions and explained life in this reformatory. Here the inmates were required to complete their high school education, attend chapel, and learn a marketable trade.*

*The training these boys received while incarcerated at the Reformatory was all-encompassing. The Reformatory grew their own vegetables, raised their own meat, chopped their wood for heating, baked their own bread, and maintained the pristine grounds.*

*In fact, during the Great Depression, people would line up outside the Reformatory kitchen door hoping to receive any leftovers as the food was much better there than that offered at the local soup kitchen.*

*The inmates also received instructions about what was expected while they lived at the Ohio State Reformatory. The consequences of not following the rules were severe and immediate. Forget to wear your belt or tie your shoes? No dinner tonight. Why? You weren't properly attired and prepared. Expected behavior. Definite consequences.*

*The recidivism rate, a criminal's relapse into criminal behavior after release, was dramatically low.*

By the time these inmates completed their sentence, they were able to function well in society.

As I came around the corner from solitary confinement, I happened to glance up. There supporting, yet adorning, the caged stairwell was intricately designed scrollwork. I paused, stunned by the beauty.

Even in the midst of prison, there was indescribable beauty. Not only did these inmates learn a marketable trade, they perfected it to the point of creating things of beauty within their vision.

But why would you want to make a prison look beautiful?

Perhaps their instructors saw the young inmates' potential for beauty and used these trades to cultivate and call out that inward characteristic to give them hope.

Back in my cell for the day, I begin to reflect on my own prison. Yes, at the moment I am physically in a cell, but honestly I've been living in a cell for many years.

My cell is closed in, dank, dark, tricked by glimpses of light, yet its warmth is illusive. I choose to remain shut off, hidden, locked away from possible pain.

*I built my own prison through:*

- *Angry words uttered out of fear of being exposed.*
- *Selfish actions meant to protect my damaged heart.*
- *Pitiful grasps to control all aspects of my life and my emotions.*

*My prison had its own rules:*

- *Do everything so well no one can find any fault.*
- *Don't offend anyone for any reason ever.*
- *Dominate your environment.*
- *Deny emotional attachments which will only bring pain.*

*Yet, these rules do not promise freedom. They only serve to strengthen the bars and cinch down the chain.*

*I am here of my own choosing.*

*Strangely, I'm comfortable within these bars. And that disturbs me.*

*For most of my adult life I've believed:*

- *I wasn't good enough, or pretty enough, or smart enough, or rich enough, or talented enough, or whatever enough.*

- *I wasn't a good person — too stubborn, opinionated, and direct.*
- *I was a failure because I'd tried something bold and audacious and didn't succeed like I'd planned.*
- *I was invisible.*

*I sit in this cell ashamed, and embarrassed at the lies I've believed about myself.*

*My prison bars aren't physical, but they are still real.*

*I realize it is time. Time to break through. Break out. Time to choose. Time to step from the shadows back into the light.*

*The warmth of the light reminds me the Truth is very different from my prison of lies. In fact, the Truth is diametrically opposed to these lies.*

*Yes, I'm opinionated and stubborn, but my Heavenly Father says He rejoices over me with singing.[4]*

*Yes, I may not be deemed a beauty in the world's eyes, but He says I am wonderfully created.[5]*

*Yes, I've failed often, and will continue to do so, but He says He has a perfect hope and future[6] for me.*

*Yes, I may not be well known, but He says He calls me by name[7] and knows me.*

*God's Truth says:*

- *You and I are unique and the world needs our uniqueness.*
- *You and I are special and have much to offer.*
- *You and I are smart enough.*
- *You and I have unlimited potential to change the world for the better.*
- *You and I are incredibly valuable.*
- *You and I can choose compassion over control.*
- *You and I are made in God's image and are therefore creative.*
- *You and I are held in God's hand.*
- *You and I have the choice to break free from the lies.*

*My choice, as I sit in this cell, is:*
*to turn around and walk through the open door, or*
*close the door once again and remain trapped in these lies.*

*The door to my prison is open. The choice is mine. Lies or Truth?*

*I leave that cell, walk back to the chapel, and sit in the quiet.*

# When Grace Wins

*See what great love the Father has lavished on us, that we should be called children of God! And that is what we are!*

1 John 3:1

"We have an enemy, and it's not each other,'" writes Lysa TerKeurst in her book, *Uninvited*. It took many years to learn this, but now we stand on this truth. That perfect world I'd spent my life desiring pales in comparison to our new, truth-filled life. The fairy tale world no longer sparkles alluringly.

Instead of a fairy tale "perfect" marriage we now have a healthy marriage rebuilt on trust, truth, and transparency.

- We still struggle. But now we have knowledge to combat the struggle.
- We still argue. But now we have tools to help us quickly resolve the issue.
- I still live with depression. But now I know the warning signs so I can capture my thoughts before I enter the spin cycle.

- He still struggles with maintaining a pure mind. But now he knows his triggers, so he can identify them and turn to truth instead.
- We still make mistakes daily. But now we can extend grace because we know how much grace and forgiveness we've each received.

We've learned the beauty of living this day. Not that we do it perfectly, but:

- Today we laugh more quickly.
- Today we accept conflict as a normal part of healthy life.
- Today I am free from the abuse memories.
- Today we love more fiercely and honestly.
- Today we protect our time to just be together.
- Today we celebrate our uniqueness, understanding the richness it brings to our marriage.
- Today we have each other's backs. Always.
- Today we are fully alive in Christ.

He is truly my best friend, and I am his.

We both know we can completely trust the other.

We know that the prison we'd lived in for so many years no longer has control over us. It is our choice to step into freedom. It is our choice to live abundantly.

*Therefore, as God's chosen people, holy and dearly loved, clothe yourselves with compassion, kindness, humility, gentleness and patience. Bear with each other and forgive one another if any of you has a grievance against someone.*

*Forgive as the Lord forgave you. And over all these virtues
put on love, which binds them all together in perfect unity.*[2]

Nearly a decade later, I make these same choices every
single day. Sometimes I make them without even thinking
about it, but other times it's like walking a high wire above
the Grand Canyon. It takes total, mental focus.

With this healing comes the hope of a new legacy. A legacy
defined by grace, peace, and encouragement. A legacy built
brick by brick with God's Truth instead of my prison of lies.

Love is a verb, an act of my will.

Today, I choose to keep my word, my covenant vow.
Today I choose to live.
Today I choose freedom.

Together we are writing a new legacy of honesty and grace.
Together we are choosing a way out.

# Appendix

# The ABC's of My Position

## I am...

Accepted in the Beloved - Ephesians 1:6
Bought with a Price - 1 Corinthians 6:20
Crucified with Christ - Galatians 2:20
Dwelt by the Holy Spirit - 1 Corinthians 3:16
Enslaved to God - Romans 6:22
Freed from slavery to sin - Romans 6:18
God's Child - Romans 8:14
Heir of God's Riches - Galatians 4:6-7
In Him Complete - Colossians 2:10
Jesus' chosen inheritance - Ephesians 1:4
Kingly Priest - 1 Peter 2:9
Light of the World - Matthew 5:14
Mastered no longer by Sin - Romans 6:14
New Creation - 2 Corinthians 5:14
One spirit with the Lord - 1 Corinthians 6:17
Perfect in Christ - Hebrews 10:14
Quieted in the reality of who God is - Psalm 46:10
Raised up with Him - Ephesians 2:5-6
Seated in Heavenly places with Christ - Ephesians 2:5-6
Transformed into the image of Christ - 2 Corinthians 3:18
United to the Lord - 1 Corinthians 6:17
Victorious through my Lord - 1 Corinthians 15:57
Wonderfully made - Psalm 139:14
Xpistos (greek for Christ) workmanship - Ephesians 2:10
Yoked with righteousness - 2 Corinthians 6:14
Zealous for good works - Titus 2:14

*Used with Permission. Your Secret Name by Kary Oberbrunner. Grand Rapids: Zondervan, 2010.*

# Depression Signs and Symptoms

Depression is more than "the blues." It is more than having a down day or feeling sad. Depression is a real disease. There is help available to you. And there is no shame in asking for help.

If you suspect someone you love is depressed, encourage them to seek medical help. Offer to go with them to the doctor or hospital. Let them know you care about their health and are willing to support them in their recovery.

If you think you may be depressed, a good place to start might be to take the online depression test at www. depressedtest.com/

According to the National Institute of Mental Health, symptoms of depression may include the following:

- Difficulty concentrating, remembering details, and making decisions
- Fatigue and decreased energy
- Feelings of guilt, worthlessness, and/or helplessness
- Feelings of hopelessness and/or pessimism
- Insomnia, early-morning wakefulness, or excessive sleeping
- Irritability, restlessness
- Loss of interest in activities or hobbies once pleasurable, including sex

- Overeating or appetite loss
- Persistent aches or pains, headaches, cramps, or digestive problems that do  not ease even with treatment
- Persistent sad, anxious, or "empty" feelings
- Thoughts of suicide, suicide attempts

*(Excerpted from WebMD.com)*

## Signs of Walking Depression

What is "walking depression"? Depression has many different faces. The most common symptoms of clinical depression are listed above. The person who may be suffering from walking depression may exhibit the following symptoms:

- Nothing is fun—you don't look forward to anything
- Can't find flow—no joy in working on a creative project
- Low energy level—you are just plain tired
- Simmering resentment toward others—other's happiness makes you bitter
- Caustic self-talk—heavy reliance on shame to motivate yourself
- Deprive yourself of creative work time—gives you a perverse sense of control and suffering
- Significant mood changes when consuming caffeine or alcohol—either hyper-optimistic or very mellow
- Feel like you are wasting your life—asking what the purpose is in what you are doing

*(Excerpted from http://gresik.ca/2012/03/10-signs-of-walking-depression/*
*Read the entire article to gain a better understanding of Walking Depression.)*

# Warnings Signs for Suicide

Depression carries a high risk of suicide. Anybody who expresses suicidal thoughts or intentions should be taken very, very seriously. Do not hesitate to call your local suicide hotline immediately.

Call 1-800-SUICIDE (1-800-784-2433) or 1-800-273-TALK (1-800-273-8255)—or the deaf hotline at 1-800-799-4TTY (1-800-799-4889).

Warning signs of suicide with depression include:

- A sudden switch from being very sad to being very calm or appearing to be happy
- Always talking or thinking about death
- Clinical depression (deep sadness, loss of interest, trouble sleeping and eating) that gets worse
- Having a "death wish," tempting fate by taking risks that could lead to death, such as driving through red lights
- Losing interest in things one used to care about
- Making comments about being hopeless, helpless, or worthless
- Putting affairs in order, tying up loose ends, changing a will
- Saying things like "It would be better if I wasn't here" or "I want out"
- Talking about suicide (killing one's self)
- Visiting or calling people one cares about

*(excerpted from helpguide.org: http://bit.ly/2kygQso. Accessed December 6, 2016.)*

# Where Can You Find Help For Depression?

**Contact your local doctor or hospital immediately when someone you know is suicidal.**

Once the crisis is under control, seek out a counselor in your area. If you don't know where to start, contact one of the following who will assist you or direct you to someone in your area.

New Life Individual & Family Services
214.772.4628

Christian Counsel
Rob Jackson
888.891.HOPE

Wings of Hope Counseling Center
Julie Dozier, LPC-S
wingscounseling.com

# Who Can I Call For Help?

**This book is not intended as a substitute for the medical advice of physicians or counseling by a licensed counselor. The reader should regularly consult a physician in matters relating to his or her health and particularly with respect to any symptoms that may require diagnosis or medical attention.**

**Material presented in this book and appendix is intended for information purposes only. It is not intended as professional advice and should not be construed as such.**

1. As always, if there is immediate danger, call 9-1-1
2. If danger is not immediate, call your family doctor for an appointment
3. If you'd like to spend more time on your own exploring, you may consult these resources I've identified through various online searches. I have no immediate knowledge of these companies and their services. These are simply places to start in your quest to find healing.

**National Suicide Prevention Center**
1-800-273-8255 (1-800-273-TALK)

## The National Domestic Violence Hotline
Immediate danger, call 9-1-1
1-800-799-7233
1-800-787-3224 (TTY)

## Celebrate Hope
Christian Drug and Alcohol Treatment Center
1-800-708-3173

## ChristianCounsel
Rob Jackson, MS, LPC
ChristianCounsel
888.891.HOPE
www.ChristianCounsel.com

## Hope by the Sea
Alcohol and Drug Treatment Programs
1-844-281-7131

## Behavioral Health of the Palm Beaches
Christian Alcohol and Drug Recovery
888-432-2467

## Capstone Treatment Center
Residential treatment center for young adult and adolescent
males (ages 13-25)
866-729-4479

## Covenant Hills
A Pacific Hills Treatment Center
800-662-2873
800-No-Abuse

## His High Places
Crisis and Crossroads Christian Counseling
888-963-4866

## HopeQuest Ministry Group
Residential, Support Groups, Drug and Alcohol, Sexual
Addictions
866-377-7589

## Marble Retreat
Christian Leader Renewal Center
970-963-2499

## Penfield Christian Homes
Addiction Ministry
1-866-KICKDRUGS
866-542-5378

## The Center - A Place of Hope
Christian Counseling for Depression, Anxiety, Disorders,
and Addictions
1-888-771-5166

## Timberline Knolls
Christian Residential Treatment Center Depression, Anxiety,
Disorders, Trauma, and Addictions
1-866-572-5380

## Selah House
Eating disorder treatment for females, ages 12 and older
1-888-692-0505

## Galaxy Recovery
Faith-based Addiction recovery
1-855-712-9441

## The Ranch
Treatment for Trauma, Abuse, Disorders, Drug and Alcohol
rehab
888-503-1801

## Renewal: Christian Treatment and Recovery
Depression, Addiction, Disorders
888-298-HOPE (4673)

## The Christian Treatment Center
Depression, Anxiety, Drug and Alcohol treatment
877-443-7342

## American Addiction Centers
Addiction and Co-Occurring Disorders
1-888-970-9446

## The Watershed Addiction Treatment Programs
Alcohol and Drug Addiction
1-844-550-7763

## Wings of Hope Counseling
Relationship Counseling, Sexual Addiction, and more
www.wingscounseling.com

# Signs Someone You Love Is Addicted

When we first reached out for help, we were told there had been signs of the pornography addiction. I had ignored those signs either out of ignorance or refusal to admit what I was seeing.

Not everyone will exhibit every sign, but if someone you love is exhibiting any of these behaviors, be bold enough to ask some tough questions. Then seek professional help to overcome the addiction. Remember, pornography addiction is not fatal.

According to Dr. Mark Laaser[1] you may wonder if somone you love is addicted if they:

1. **Tell you they can stop at any time.** Just like other addicts, a person addicted to porn has to admit they do not have control over it. It has taken over their life. You might hear something like, "It's okay. I can stop whenever I want. I won't do it again."

2. **Spend increasing time looking at pornography.** Similar to using drugs like heroin or cocaine, pornography triggers neurochemical reactions in the brain. Combine this with an orgasm and you have an explosive high that quickly requires more and more exposure to experience that high. Instead of

---

[1]   Dr. Mark Laaser. https://www.faithfulandtrue.com/About-Us.aspx

an occasional look, the person may now be spending hours every day looking at pornography. The easiest source is online.

3. **Exhibit degenerative behavior.** Though the addiction may start with soft porn such as *Sports Illustrated Swim Suit Issue* or *Victoria's Secret Catalog*, the person addicted to porn will need more hard-core pornography to get the same high.

4. **Neglect relationships.** The addiction will eventually affect every area of the addict's life. Marriage problems will develop. Emotionally the addict will experience loneliness, fear, guilt, shame, anxiety, secrecy, fatigue, and low self-esteem. Most addicts know what they are doing is wrong and harmful to their relationships.

5. **Are obviously self-medicating.** Addicts use porn to self-medicate similar to other drug addicts. Self-medicating relates to some deep pain or wound that the person feels incapable of dealing with.

6. **Exhibit narcissistic behavior.** Someone suffering from an addiction is focusing on their own needs or wants. They tend to be self-focused and believe they are entitled to do whatever they want whenever they want completely discounting how their behavior and actions affect those they love.

7. **Justify negative behavior.** Any of us can justify our behavior if we work at it. One of the ways we do that is to say that because we've worked hard and performed well, we get a reward. Addicts often justify their behavior with this logic.

8. **Believe their behavior creates power.** At the root of most addictions is the feeling of

powerlessness in one or more areas of your life. Using porn or any other addictive behavior gives the addict a false sense of control and power.

*(Excerpted from Peter Kleponis's article "8 Characteristics of Porn Addiction". http://www.covenanteyes.com/2015/11/117/8-characteristics-of-porn-addiction/. For a complete explanation, visit this website.)*

# Questions To Ask If You Think Someone You Love Is Addicted To Pornography

One of the questions I asked early in our counseling was why I didn't know about the pornography addiction. Looking back, I realize I did know about it—I just didn't want to acknowledge the signs.

Here are a few questions to ask yourself if you are suspicious about a sexual addiction.

1. Are they being secretive?
2. Has their desire for sexual intimacy decreased or do they seem distant or preoccupied in your presence?
3. Do they expect you to participate in unusual or odd sexual activity against your consent?
4. If you approach them, do they quickly turn off or shutdown their computer?
5. Have they been spending more time than usual on the internet?
6. Are they working a lot of late nights?
7. Are there unexplained financial abnormalities?
8. Is the person critical of your physical appearance?

A great resource on this subject is an article by Matt Fradd: *10 Signs of Porn Addiction: Do these describe your husband?* http://bit.ly/2jCx5Rn

# Inner Healing
# Guidelines

1. **IDENTIFYING & FEELING THE EMOTION**
Jesus, what recurring emotion have I been struggling with? Please help me feel the emotion.

2. **DISCOVERING THE ROOT EVENT**
God, when was the first time I experienced this emotion?

3. **DISCERNING THE LIE BELIEVED**
Jesus, what did I come to believe?

4. **REVEALING THE TRUTH**
Lord, what truth do You have to communicate with me about the lie?

5. **EXPERIENCING HIS FREEDOM**
If healing has occurred, you should sense new freedom from the bondage. If bondage remains, is there another lie, Lord? If you are blocked, steps 6-10 may be helpful.

6. **DISCOVERING WHAT JESUS WAS DOING**
Jesus, what were You doing and feeling when the wounding event took place?

7. **EXTENDING & RECEIVING FORGIVENESS**
Jesus, have I forgiven the one who hurt me? God, have I forgiven myself? Have I come to peace with You for allowing it?

8. **UNCOVERING & RENOUNCING VOWS**
Lord, is there a vow I made to protect myself from pain? If so, renounce it and cancel it in Jesus' name.

9. **BREAKING ANY PRONOUNCEMENTS**
God, did an authority make a pronouncement over me? If so, break it in Jesus' name.

10. **SURRENDERING A BURDEN TO JESUS**
If Jesus would take your burden, would you be willing to surrender it to Him? If you give the burden to Him, what will He give you in return? Gather the burden and lay it at His feet. What does Jesus do with the burden?

*The Sovereign Lord...has sent Me to heal the brokenhearted and to announce that captives will be released and prisoners will be freed...To all who mourn...He will give beauty for ashes, joy instead of mourning, praise instead of despair... Isaiah 61:1-3*

# Listening to God Guidelines

1. **COME FULLY PRESENT BEFORE GOD**
   Fix your attention fully on Jesus and away from distractions. Hebrews 12:2

2. **EXERCISE CHRIST'S AUTHORITY OVER ALL OTHER VOICES**
   Pray similar to, "In the name of Jesus Christ, I command all other voices to be silent." James 4:7 and Acts 16:18

3. **ASK THE THREE-IN-ONE TO REVEAL HIMSELF IN A SPECIAL WAY**
   "Come quickly to rescue and help me, O Lord." Psalm 70:1

4. **ASK GOD TO SEARCH YOUR HEART**
   Talk to Him about what He reveals, confess any known sin. Psalm 139:23-24

5. **ASK JESUS TO COMMUNICATE WITH YOU**
   Speak, Lord, for I am listening. 1 Samuel 3:10 and John 16:12-14

6. **WAIT IN SILENCE**
   My soul waits in silence for God only. Psalm 62:1

7. **WRITE DOWN IMPRESSIONS**
   Usually this will be thoughts, pictures, or Scripture that enters your heart and mind. 1 Corinthians 2:10-16

8. **TEST IMPRESSIONS WITH GOD'S WORD, HIS CHARACTER & THE BODY OF CHRIST**
   Don't suppress the Spirit or stifle God's communication, but don't be gullible. Check it out carefully; keep only what passes the test. 1 Thessalonians 5:19-22

# How To Journal

Journaling is simply putting words on paper. There's no correct formula, book, ink color, or even topic.

Journaling is first and foremost personal.

Here's a few quick tips to help you get started.

1. **Get a notebook.** Any notebook. Seriously, the kind of notebook doesn't matter.
2. **Set aside a location.** Where are you the most comfortable? Some people create a special space to journal. I have a comfortable chair where I read my Bible and journal.
3. **Start.** The hardest part about journaling is starting. Therefore, pick a day to start and just do it. Here's a couple of starting points for you:

    ◆ What problem is on your mind?
    ◆ What is something special that happened in the last 24 hours?
    ◆ What did you think about what you read in the Bible?
    ◆ What do you just need to "talk out"?

4. **Be consistent.** Write something in your journal often, every day if possible and about the same time of day. However, if you skip a day, don't give up. The

discipline of writing in your journal consistently will ingrain the habit. Pretty soon, you'll find you are journaling without having to make a conscious effort.

5. **Keep it private.** Your journal is for your eyes only. Therefore, you can write whatever you want in it. If you're having a rough day, go ahead and have your rant in your journal. You'll feel better when you do. If you have young children or others in your home you feel might be tempted to pick it up and read it, go ahead and put it someplace it won't be easily found.

6. **Forget about grammar and punctuation rules.** Remember, this is for you. Just write your thoughts, disjointed as they may be at times.

7. **Write the date the prayer was answered next to the prayer.** If you write some of your prayers, when that prayer is answered go back and write the date of the answer next to the original prayer. I've found this to be very encouraging.

8. **Write about what is comfortable to you.** My journaling started out very simply. I talked mostly about momentous occasions or special things that happened in a day. Sometimes it was a funny quote from one of my kids. But as I developed my journaling muscle, my entries changed and morphed into more reflection type entries.

9. **There's no set amount of writing you need to do.** It doesn't matter if you write one sentence, one paragraph, one page, or 30 pages in a day. Each day will vary in length and that's okay. Keep practicing.

10. **Enjoy the process.** Honestly, I never thought I'd find journaling therapeutic. However, it is. I've even been known to grab my journal and have a major meltdown. When I'm done with my rant, I feel better. And no one got hurt in the process.

Remember, journaling is very personal. Develop your way of doing it and enjoy.

## Beginning Journal Exercise

How do you start to journal? If you're like me, you just jump in and it doesn't look too pretty. Nothing fancy. Nothing official. A spiral bound notebook like the ones from your school days works just fine.

You just start to write. If pen scares you and feels too permanent, hunt down a pencil. If you think better while you type, feel free to peck away at your keyboard. There is no "right" way.

Start with this simple exercise. Fill in your thoughts for numbers 1-5 each day for one week.

1. Today I feel:
2. When I feel this way the thoughts that go through my head are:
3. When I feel this way and think these thoughts, I want to:
4. My choice today is to:
5. My prayer today is:

This is for you. Don't strive for perfection. You don't need the "right" words. This will not be laminated and passed around to a judge and jury. This is between you and God. Give your mind, heart, and soul a little attention each day. Give God the opportunity to love on you and redirect your day and your gaze.

# Helpful Questions
# To Ask Each Other

Just as in life, every marriage has seasons.

There are seasons when your marriage feels exceptional. You are in sync together, dreaming together, and thoroughly enjoying your relationship.

There are seasons where life is so busy you barely have time to connect. You know the other person was home because their side of the bed is messed up. But communication consists of quick text messages or phone calls. You might get 15 minutes to eat together once a day before one or both of you are on to the next event — your child's sporting event, a new business client meeting, church meeting, or volunteer activity. Watch for warning signs during this season.

There is the season when it feels like you've become roommates. Gone is the romance and maybe even the desire to spend time together. You barely talk unless it's about the children. You are rarely alone together and neither one of you misses the other. This is a dangerous time for your marriage.

Here's some questions[1] you can ask each other during each season of your marriage. Listen carefully to each other. Your

---

[1]  http://guidedoc.com/20-helpful-marriage-counseling-questions-ask-spouse accessed on 12.13.16

answers will help you protect and build your marriage into the best it can be.

- What are our main issues?
- What issues do you think are most important?
- How are we doing with our relationship?
- Are we going through a bad phase or is it something more?
- What do I do that bothers you or makes you feel "less than"?
- Do you love me? If so, what kind of love is it?
- Do you trust me?
- Are you satisfied with our sex life?
- Do you feel accepted by me?
- Do we have anything between us that we still need to resolve?
- Is there anything you need to tell me?
- Are you considering a divorce?
- Do we need to get counseling?

Marriage counseling is a good thing. Even "good" marriages can use some unbiased evaluation from time to time.

According to gotquestions.org,[1] when there are recurring issues, such as those listed below, counseling is very wise:

- Unable to resolve conflict in a healthy way
- One partner dominates the relationship so the other's needs aren't met
- Lack of compromise

---

[1] http://www.gotquetions.org "When should a Christian couple seek marriage counseling" accessed on 12.15.16

- Communication breaks down
- One partner seeks to "fix" a problem outside of the marriage
- Role confusion
- Pornography
- Lying by one or the other spouse
- Parenting styles don't jive
- Addictions or addictive behavior

If you find yourself dealing with some of these issues, reach out to a good Christian counseling agency in your area. Your church will be a good resource for counselors in your area.

# Where Can I Go To Learn More About God?

1. Read the book of John in the Bible.
2. If you don't have a Bible, go to www.biblegateway.com and type in "Book of John" in the search bar. I recommend you read it in the New International Version, THE MESSAGE, or the New Living Translation.
3. There are several apps you can download. (at the time of this writing all are free)

   A. SheReadsTruth
      Check out under plans:

      i.  "Open Your Bible//Launch-Week Sampler" (free)
      ii. "This is the Gospel" (free)

   B. YouVersion
      Check out under plans/Discover:

      i.   "Bible Introduction"
      ii.  "Finding Your Way Back to God"
      iii. "You'll Be Okay"
      iv.  "Names for God"

4. Read the book, *The Case For Christ* by Lee Strobel.

# Scripture Verses Helpful For Dealing With Depression And Anxiety

Below are several verses that helped me in my recovery from depression and anxiety. Often, I would read these over to remind myself of God's presence and care in my life.

Some of them reminded me of my need to confess my sin, repent (which means to agree with God that sin is sin), and ask for forgiveness. Meditating on God's truth combats the lies the enemy of our souls inserts daily.

I pray they will be encouragement or food for thought for you as well.

**2 Samuel 22:29**
You, LORD, are my lamp; the LORD turns my darkness into light.

**Psalm 31:9**
Be merciful to me, LORD, for I am in distress; my eyes grow weak with sorrow, my soul and body with grief.

## Psalm 32:5-7

Then I acknowledged my sin to you and did not cover up my iniquity.

I said, "I will confess my transgressions to the Lord."

And you forgave the guilt of my sin.

Therefore let all the faithful pray to you while you may be found; surely the rising of the mighty waters will not reach them.

You are my hiding place; you will protect me from trouble and surround me with songs of deliverance.

## Psalm 34:18

The LORD is close to the brokenhearted and saves those who are crushed in spirit.

## Psalm 40:11-13

Do not withhold your mercy from me, Lord; may your love and faithfulness always protect me.

For troubles without number surround me; my sins have overtaken me, and I cannot see.

They are more than the hairs of my head, and my heart fails within me.

Be pleased to save me, Lord; come quickly, Lord, to help me.

## Psalm 51:10-12

Create in me a clean heart, O God, and renew a steadfast spirit within me. Do not cast me from your presence or take your Holy Spirit from me. Restore to me the joy of your salvation and grant me a willing spirit, to sustain me.

## Psalm 61

Hear my cry, O God; listen to my prayer.

From the ends of the earth I call to you, I call as my heart grows faint; lead me to the rock that is higher than I.

For you have been my refuge, a strong tower against the foe. I long to dwell in your tent forever and take refuge in the shelter of your wings.

For you, God, have heard my vows; you have given me the heritage of those who fear your name.

Increase the days of the king's life, his years for many generations.

May he be enthroned in God's presence forever; appoint your love and faithfulness to protect him.

Then I will ever sing in praise of your name and fulfill my vows day after day.

## Psalm 90:8

You have set our iniquities before you, our secret sins in the light of your presence.

## Psalm 116

I love the Lord, for he heard my voice; he heard my cry for mercy.

Because he turned his ear to me, I will call on him as long as I live.

The cords of death entangled me, the anguish of the grave came over me; I was overcome by distress and sorrow.

Then I called on the name of the Lord: "Lord, save me!"

The Lord is gracious and righteous; our God is full of compassion.

The Lord protects the unwary; when I was brought low, he saved me.

**Psalm 119:27-29**

Cause me to understand the way of your precepts, that I may meditate on your wonderful deeds.

My soul is weary with sorrow; strengthen me according to your word.

Keep me from deceitful ways; be gracious to me and teach me your law.

**Psalm 119:96**

To all perfection I see a limit; but your commands are boundless.

**Psalm 119:151**

Yet you are near, O LORD, and all your commands are true.

**Psalm 119:153**

Look upon my suffering and deliver me, for I have not forgotten your law.

**Psalm 119:165**

Those who love your instructions have great peace and do not stumble.

**Psalm 119:169-172**

May my cry come before you, LORD; give me understanding according to your word.

May my supplication come before you; deliver me according to your promise.

May my lips overflow with praise, for you teach me your decrees.

May my tongue sing of your word, for all your commands are righteous.

**Psalm 121:2-3**

My help comes from the LORD, the Maker of heaven and earth. He will not let your foot slip—he who watches over you will not slumber;

**Psalm 121:7-8**

The LORD will keep you from harm—he will watch over your life; the LORD will watch over your coming and going both now and forevermore.

**Psalm 126:3**

The LORD has done great things for us, and we are filled with joy.

**Proverbs 18:10**

The name of the LORD is a strong fortress; the godly run to him and are safe.

**Proverbs 28:26**

He who trusts in himself is a fool, but he who walks in wisdom is kept safe.

**Isaiah 26:3**

You will keep in perfect peace him whose mind is steadfast, because he trusts in you.

**Isaiah 66:13**

As a mother comforts her child, so will I comfort you.

**Daniel 9:9**

The Lord our God is merciful and forgiving, even though we have rebelled against him.

## Micah 7:7

But as for me, I watch in hope for the LORD, I wait for God my Savior; my God will hear me.

## Zephaniah 3:17

The Lord your God is with you, the Mighty Warrior who saves.
He will take great delight in you; in his love he will no longer rebuke you, but will rejoice over you with singing.

## John 12:46

I have come into the world as a light, so that no one who believes in me should stay in darkness.

## Romans 5:1-5

Therefore, since we have been justified through faith, we have peace with God through our Lord Jesus Christ, through whom we have gained access by faith into this grace in which we now stand. And we boast in the hope of the glory of God. Not only so, but we also glory in our sufferings, because we know that suffering produces perseverance; perseverance, character; and character, hope. And hope does not put us to shame, because God's love has been poured out into our hearts through the Holy Spirit, who has been given to us.

## 2 Corinthians 10:4-5

The weapons we fight with are not the weapons of the world. On the contrary, they have divine power to demolish strongholds. We demolish arguments and every pretension that sets itself up against the knowledge of God, and we take captive every thought to make it obedient to Christ.

## Galatians 5:1

It is for freedom that Christ has set us free. Stand firm, then, and do not let yourselves be burdened again by a yoke of slavery.

## Ephesians 5:8

For you were once darkness, but now you are light in the Lord. Live as children of light

## 2 Timothy 2:19

Nevertheless, God's solid foundation stands firm, sealed with this inscription: "The Lord knows those who are his," and, "Everyone who confesses the name of the Lord must turn away from wickedness."

## 1 Peter 2:9

But you are a chosen people, a royal priesthood, a holy nation, God's special possession, that you may declare the praises of him who called you out of darkness into his wonderful light.

## 1 John 1:5-9

This is the message we have heard from him and declare to you: God is light; in him there is no darkness at all. If we claim to have fellowship with him and yet walk in the darkness, we lie and do not live out the truth. But if we walk in the light, as he is in the light, we have fellowship with one another, and the blood of Jesus, his Son, purifies us from all sin. If we claim to be without sin, we deceive ourselves and the truth is not in us. If we confess our sins, he is faithful and just and will forgive us our sins and purify us from all unrighteousness.

## 1 John 3:1

How great is the love the Father has lavished on us, that we should be called children of God! And that is what we are!

# Resources

Below is a short list of suggested resources. This is *not* an exhaustive list, merely a place to start.

## Addiction

### Restoring the Fallen
Earl & Sandy Wilson, Paul & Virginia Friesen, and Larry & Nancy Paulson.© 1997. Published by InterVarsity Press, the book publishing division of InterVarsity Christian Fellowship.

### Your Secret Name
Kary Oberbrunner.© By Kary Oberbrunner. Published by Zondervan, Grand Rapids, MI 49530.

http://www.covenanteyes.com/blog/

http://www.covenanteyes.com/2016/03/31/how-we-talk-about-porn-matters/

http://familylifetoday.com/resources/life-issues/

## Counselors

Rob Jackson, http://christianfamilyuniversity.com/counseling/

Julie Dozier, http://www.wingscounseling.com

New Life Individual & Family Services, 214.772.4628

# Daily Living

## Knowing God
J.I. Packer. © 1973 by J.I. Packer. Seventeenth American printing, December 1979, by InterVarsity Press with permission of Hodder and Stoughton Limited, London.

## Margin
Dr. Richard Swenson. © 1995, 2004 by Richard A. Swenson. Published by NavPress, P.O. Box 35001, Colorado Springs, CO 80935.

## One Thousand Gifts
Ann Voskamp. © 2010 by Ann Morton Voskamp. Published by Zondervan, Grand Rapids, MI 49530.

## The Circle Maker
Mark Batterson. © 2011 by Mark Batterson. Published by Zondervan, Grand Rapids, MI 49530.

## Scary Close
Donald Miller. © 2014 by Donald Miller. Published by Nelson Books, an imprint of Thomas Nelson. Nelson Books and Thomas Nelson are registered trademarks of HarperCollins Christian Publishing, Inc.

## Uninvited
Lysa TerKeurst. © 2016 by TerKeurst Foundation. Published by Nelson Books, an imprint of Thomas Nelson. Nelson Books and Thomas Nelson are registered trademarks of HarperCollins Christian Publishing, Inc.

## Depression & Grief

### A Grace Disguised: How The Soul Grows through Loss

By Jerry L. Sittser © 1995, 2004, by Gerald L. Sittser. Published by Zondervan, Grand Rapids, MI 49530.

### Happiness is a Choice

Frank Minirth, MD & Paul Meier, MD. © 1978, 1994, 2007, 2013 by Frank B. Minirth and Paul D. Meier. Published by Baker Books, a division of Baker Publishing Group. P.O. Box 6287, Grand Rapids, MI 49516-6287.

### The Wounded Heart

Dan Allender. © 2008 by Dan Allender. Published by NavPress, P.O. Box 35001, Colorado Springs, CO 80935.

### Straight Talk on Depression: Overcoming Emotional Battles with the Power of God's Word!

Joyce Meyer. ©2003 by Joyce Meyer. Published by FaithWords, a division of Hachette Book Group, Nashville, TN.

http://familylifetoday.com/resources/life-issues/

## Marriage

### Laugh Your Way to a Better Marriage

Mark Gungor. ©2008. Laugh Your Way America, LLC. Published by Atria Paperback, A Division of Simon & Schuster, Inc. 1230 Avenue of the Americas, New York, NY 10020.

### Healing Your Marriage When Trust is Broken: Finding Forgiveness & Restoration

Cindy Beall. © 2011 by Cindy Beall. Published by Harvest House Publishers, Eugene, OR 97402.

### Creating a Haven of Peace

Joanne Fairchild Miller. ©2016 by Joanne Fairchild Miller. Published by Morgan James Publishing, New York, NY.

### I Do Again: How We Found a Second Chance at Our Marriage—and You Can Too

Cheryl and Jeff Scruggs. ©2008 by Cheryl and Jeff Scruggs. Published by WaterBrook Press, Colorado Springs, CO 80920.

http://www.covenanteyes.com/2016/03/28/3-truths-to-help-you-heal-from-marital-betrayal/

http://loveandrespect.com/ Dr. Emerson & Sarah Eggerichs

http://familylifetoday.com/resources/marriage/

http://www.focusonthefamily.com/marriage

## Parenting

### Parenting Isn't for Cowards

Dr. James C. Dobson. © 1987. Tyndale House Publishers, Inc. Carol Stream, IL.

### The Way They Learn
Cynthia Ulrich Tobias, M. Ed. © 1994. A Focus on the Family book published by Tyndale House Publishers, Inc., Carol Stream, IL 60188.

http://familylifetoday.com/resources/parenting/

http://www.focusonthefamily.com/parenting

## Political Activism
http://endsexualexploitation.org/

## Technology
**Covenant Eyes**: Internet accountability software available for individuals or for your whole family. http://www.covenanteyes.com/

**TripleX Church accountability software**: Internet accountability software available for individuals
http://bit.ly/2kpxnvy

# Endnotes

## When Grace Begins

1 Zechariah 9:12 New Living Translation.

## When You Stumble Over What's Hidden

1 Psalm 34:8-10 New International Version.

## When You Step In It

1 http://www.madmagazine.com/

2 Sam Black, The Porn Circuit, (Owosso: Covenant Eyes, Inc., 2013), PDF e-book, http://www.covenanteyes.com/science-of-porn-addiction-ebook/, 6.

## When It's Not So Happily Ever After

1 Sam Black, *The Porn Circuit*, (Owosso: Covenant Eyes, Inc., 2013), PDF e-book, http://www.covenanteyes.com/science-of-porn-addiction-ebook/, 9.

2 Sam Black, *The Porn Circuit*, (Owosso: Covenant Eyes, Inc., 2013), PDF e-book, http://www.covenanteyes.com/science-of-porn-addiction-ebook/, 25.

## When Friends Believe For You

1   Earl & Sandy Wilson, Paul & Virginia Friesen, Larry & Nancy Paulson, *Restoring the Fallen: A Team Approach to Caring, Confronting, & Reconciling*, (Downers Grove: InterVarsity Press, 1997).

## When You Make The Team You Don't Want

1   Earl & Sandy Wilson, Paul & Virginia Friesen, Larry & Nancy Paulson, *Restoring the Fallen: A Team Approach to Caring, Confronting, & Reconciling*, (Downers Grove: InterVarsity Press, 1997).

## When It Starts With Commitment

1   Wilson et al, *Restoring the Fallen*, 36-37.

2   1 John 1:9 New International Version.

3   Wilson et al, *Restoring the Fallen*, 42, 44.

## When You Realize Commitment Means You Have No Control

1   Dave M. Carder and R. Duncan Jaenicke, *Torn Asunder*, (Chicago: Moody Publishers, 1992, 1995, 2008), 76.

## When You Have To Decide If You Do Or You Don't

1   Shannon Etheridge, *Every Woman's Battle: Discovering God's Plan for Sexual and Emotional Fulfillment*, (Colorado Springs: Waterbrook Press, 2003), 37.

2   Matthew 5:28 New International Version.

3   Stephen R. Covey, *The 7 Habits of Highly Effective People: Powerful Lessons in Personal Change*, (New York: Simon & Schuster, 1989, 2004), 87.

## When You Discover You Were Never Alone

1   The Navigators, "Listening and Healing Prayer Guidelines", http://shaw.navigators.org/shaw.navigators.org/media/ Documents?Five%20Smooth%20Stones/%233%20Into%20 the20%Light%20Studies/Bookmark-Listening-and-Healing-Pr ayer.pdf?_ga=1.253590977.955193728.1459461063, accessed August 12, 2016.

## When You Are Pointing A Finger In The Wrong Direction

1   Daniel 9:23 (The Message).

## When You Rip Off The Scab

1   Ephesians 5:12-14 New International Version.

## When You Are Surprised By Kindness

1   Jerry Sittser, *A Grace Disguised: Expanded Edition,* (Grand Rapids: Zondervan, 1995, 2004), 158.

## When Nothing Makes Sense

1   "Depression Signs and Symptoms", http://www.helpguide. org/articles/depression/depression-signs-and-symptoms.htm, accessed August 14, 2016.

2   Ibid.

3   Romans 8:28 New International Version.

## When Death Smacks You In The Face

1   Eaec.org, "D.L. Moody", http://www.eaec.org/faithhallfame/ dlmoody.htm, accessed August 15, 2016.

2   Shiva.com, "Sitting Shiva", http://www.shiva.com/ learning-center/sitting-shiva/, accessed August 15, 2016.

## When Too Much Happens At Once

1   Haus Am Moos, http://www.ammoos.at/en-home.htm, accessed August 20, 2016.

## When Jesus Redeems Your Past

1   Dan Allender, *The Wounded Heart: Hope of Adult Victims of Childhood Sexual Abuse,* (Colorado Springs: NavPress, 1990, 1995), 54.

## When You Learn To Grieve

1   Dan Allender, *The Wounded Heart,* 13

2   Melanie Haiken, "The 5 Stages of Grief", https://www.caring.com/articles/stages-of-grief, accessed August 20, 2016.

3   Isaiah 66:13a New International Version.

## When Unresolved Issues Reveal The Darkness

1   Psalm 40:11-13 New International Version.

2   Psalm 58:6 New International Version.

3   Psalm 35:26 New International Version.

4   Psalm 55:4 New International Version.

## When The Answer Comes At The Bottom

1   Mark 9:32 New International Version.

2   Sam Black, *The Porn Circuit,* (Owosso: Covenant Eyes, Inc., 2013), PDF e-book, http://www.covenanteyes.com/science-of-porn-addiction-ebook/, 40

## When Hurt Becomes Healing

1   Jenny Heckman, "Healthy Emotions," *Just Between Us Magazine,* Spring 2016.

2   Psalm 10:10-11 New International Version.

3 Lamentations 3:22-23 New International Version.

4 Donald Miller, *Scary Close*, (Nashville: Nelson books, an imprint of Thomas Nelson, 2014), 225.

5 X3watch accountability software. See appendix for details.

6 Covenant Eyes Software. See appendix for details.

## When Beauty Awakens

I Romans 5:1-5 New International Version.

## When You Are Completely Known And Fully Loved

I Galatians 5:1 New International Version.

2 Romans 8:1 New International Version.

3 Jeremiah 17:9 New International Version.

## When You Choose To Begin Again

I Jerry Sittser, *A Grace Revealed*, 20.

2 Matthew 7:3 New International Version.

3 Bethany and Nathan Gaddis, "Testimonies of Covenant Marriages", *Covenant Eyes, Inc.*, http://covenantmarriage.com/testimonies. Accessed September 23, 2016.

## When You Realize Covenant Is More Than A Contract

I "What is a Marriage Covenant?," *Covenant Marriage Movement*, http://covenantmarriage.com/what-is-a-marriage-covenant. Accessed September 23, 2016.

2 Matthew 5:32 New International Version.

3 Matthew 19:8 New International Version.

4 Ephesian 5:25 New International Version.

5   Dennis and Barbara Rainey, *Staying Close: Stopping the Natural Drift Toward Isolation in Marriage*, (Nashville: Thomas Nelson, Inc., 2003), 81.

## When You Learn To Take Him At His Word
1   Proverbs 19:13; Proverbs 21:9, 19; Proverbs 25:24; Proverbs 27:15 New International Version.
2   1 Peter 5:7 New International Version.
3   Psalm 55 New International Version.
4   2 Kings 10:31 New Living Translation
5   1 Peter 5:10 New International Version.
6   See Appendix A - Who Am I in Christ?

## When Your Trust Is Tested
1   2 Corinthians 10:5 New International Version.

## When You Choose Integrity
1   Doug Weiss, *Clean, A Proven Plan for Men Committed to Sexual Integrity*, (Nashville: Thomas Nelson, Inc., 2013), 97.
2   Dave M. Carder and R. Duncan Jaenicke, *Torn Asunder,* (Chicago: Moody Publishers, 1992, 1995, 2008), 121.

## When You Choose The Open Door
1   Kary Oberbrunner, "Escaping Shawshank," http://www.escapingshawshank.com/, accessed on 1.5.17
2   Steven Pressfield, *Do The Work!* (Irvington: Do You Zoom, Inc., The Domino Project, 2011), 9.
3   The Ohio State Reformatory, http://www.mrps.org, accessed August 28, 2016.
4   Zephaniah 3:17 New International Version.
5   Psalm 139:14 New International Version.

6    Jeremiah 29:11 New International Version.

7    Isaiah 43:1; John 10:27 New International Version.

## When Grace Wins

1    Lysa TerKeurst, *Uninvited: Living Loved When You Feel Less Than, Left Out, and Lonely*, (Nashville: Nelson Books, an imprint of Thomas Nelson. Nelson Books and Thomas Nelson are registered trademarks of HarperCollins Christian Publishing, Inc., 2016), 71.

2    Colossians 3:12-14 New International Version.

# Acknowledgements

No book gets written in isolation. In fact, this book would never have been written if it weren't for one comment by our counselor, "I wish everybody had the support you guys have. I hope you're writing this down. Others need to know this process and that restoration itself is possible." Well, here it is, Rob.

Thanks to our Restoration Team: Peter & Debbie Udall, Rick & Cathy Roberts, and Ken & Jackie Palmer. There are no words to adequately express what you've done for us and what you mean to us. Dave and I are who we are today because of your love and care. Love you.

Thank you, Sara Plott, for your creative editing and unrelenting demand to tell the story with emotion. You are an important part of this work. Without you, I'd still be deleting sections because they were too hard to write. Your constant encouragement to write it so others will have hope kept me going when I wanted to quit. You rock, girlfriend!

Thanks to my coach, and mentor, Kary Oberbrunner, who believed it was time to tell this story. Your constant encouragement, correction, and exhortation brought this story to print. I'm thankful God brought you into my life to light my soul on fire.

Thank you to my children and children-in-love, Erin, Casey, Eric, Emily, Nate, and Sasha, for your constant love and support of Dad and me. You believed our recovery was possible before we did and you walked the journey with us. Love you more than words can express. I am proud to be your mom. Together we are creating a new legacy.

And, finally, thank you, Dave, for being more interested in loving God than staying stuck. Thank you for doing the hard work with me to redefine and restore our marriage. Thank you for walking through the pit with me and believing healing was possible. Thank you for celebrating each day together, amazed and grateful for God's restoration. Here's to at least 100 more years together. You are my best friend, confidante, and safe place. I love you more today than ever.

# About The Author

Kirsten believes the little moments in everyday life become the legacy we leave. She attempts to greet each new day with a helpful reminder to "live your legacy today." Through her blogging, books, and coaching she helps the disheartened rediscover their unique purpose so they can boldly face the everyday challenges in life with confidence, creativity, and, hopefully, a few chuckles.

She believes that life is a lot like a sloppy, jam covered hug from a toddler. The ultimate joy is worth the mess.

Kirsten and her husband enjoy their messy life and leaving legacies together in sunny Colorado. You can connect with her at www.KirstenDSamuel.com.

# let's stay connected

www.KirstenDSamuel.com

# are you looking for hope?

You are not alone! The enemy of your soul wants you to believe the lie that no one else struggles in their marriage, in taking their thoughts captive, or in overcoming addictive behavior.

Dave & Kirsten understand. Though they are not counselors, as coaches, they will walk with you on your journey to wholeness.

If you'd like to connect with them, go to kirstendsamuel.com/coaching.

# the deeper path experience

**"People lose their way,
when they lose their why."**
Gail Hyatt

Do you know why you exist?
Do you need to discover or define your passion?
Are you tired of feeling like you have no purpose?
Do you feel wounded and wonder if you can recover?

If you are asking
yourself any of these
questions, you can
find your way to a
fulfilling life!

It is possible, and I'm
here to help.

Join me on The Deeper Path Experience and we will
walk through a proven process to discover your why
and re-engage with your direction and purpose.

Visit www.KirstenDSamuel.com/coaching for more
information and discover how strong you really are.

Certified to teach this course is based on the book, *The Deeper Path*, by Kary Oberbrunner.
Published by Baker Books. Used by permission

**Also by Kirsten Samuel**

Available at Amazon.com and other retailers in Kindle format, e-pub, paperback, hard cover, and audio book.

Made in the USA
Columbia, SC
11 November 2021